A WOOD OF ONE'S OWN

'By the end . . . I came to believe that she really did it and, briefly, that I could do it myself.'

The Sunday Times

'Draws together childhood memories, local history . . . and literary penumbra.'

Sunday Telegraph

'Pavey's unassuming memoir celebrates the imperfections of rural life and the virtues of spontaneity . . . the nonbravura style makes this book – attractively illustrated with Pavey's black-and-white sketches – a winner.'

Kate Kellaway, *Observer*

'Pavey's love for her small patch of land shimmers off the page [in this] narrative of warmth, honesty and great spirit – made all the more beautiful by Pavey's own lively and accomplished drawings . . . this lovely book is itself a gift – encouraging country-dweller and townie alike to marvel at the infinite possibilities at the heart of a single tree.'

The Daily Mail, Book of the Week

'The satisfactions are many . . . her book is a gentle, generous extension of that . . . one all her readers can share in.'

he Lady

A WOOD
of
ONE'S OWN

WRITTEN AND ILLUSTRATED BY

Ruth Pavey

DUCKWORTH

This edition first published in the United Kingdom by Duckworth in 2019

Duckworth, an imprint of Prelude Books Ltd.
13 Carrington Road, Richmond
TW10 5AA, United Kingdom
www.duckworthbooks.co.uk
www.preludebooks.co.uk

For bulk and special sales please contact info@preludebooks.co.uk

A catalogue record for this book is available from the British Library

Text design and typesetting by Tetragon, London
Printed and bound by Clays

9780715653678

To everyone who has helped,
or is still helping,
in the wood

Top of Wheat field

Larch

Cedar

Best Snowdrops

Higher Ashw

Hazel Wood

Oak

unidentified Conifers

Micket

New Pear Tree

Walnuts

Quince

New Fruit Trees

Rollalong Drive

Wild Plum Trees

Butt Ga

Bramble Willow

Pond

Rollalong Clearing

Rollalong

Old Apple First Tree

New Hedge

Damson

Suggs Orchard

Marsh

Ditch

Willows

Wheat field

Track

Ted's Orch

ROUGH PLAN of THE WOOD
(Sugg's Orchard & Long Hill Orchard)
Aller, Somerset

ckthorn

nbeam

Holly

'Hermitage'

New Apple Trees

Ashwood where the crows nest

Lost Boundary

Thicket

Rounded Slope

New Plum Trees

Long Hill Orchard

afted Apple Trees

Old Apple Trees

Boundary Walk

Boundary marking Ash

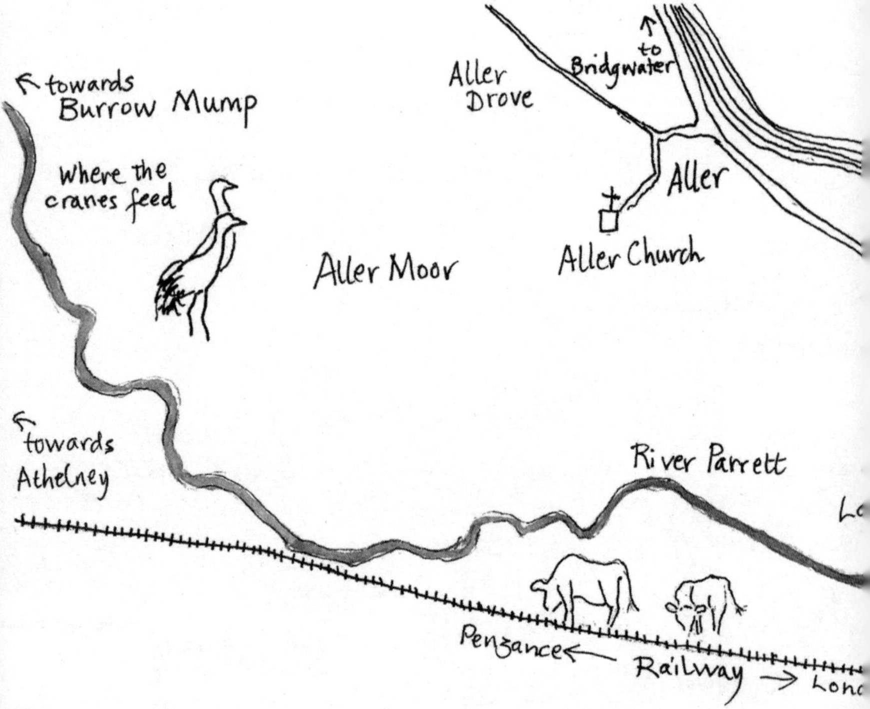

towards
Burrow Mump

Where the
cranes feed

Aller Moor

Aller
Drove

to
Bridgwater

Aller

Aller Church

towards
Athelney

River Parrett

Lo

Penzance← Railway →Lond

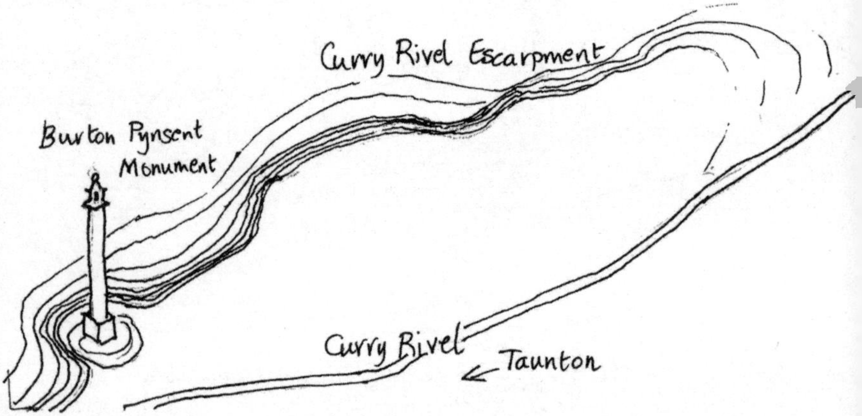

Curry Rivel Escarpment

Burton Pynsent
Monument

Curry Rivel ←Taunton

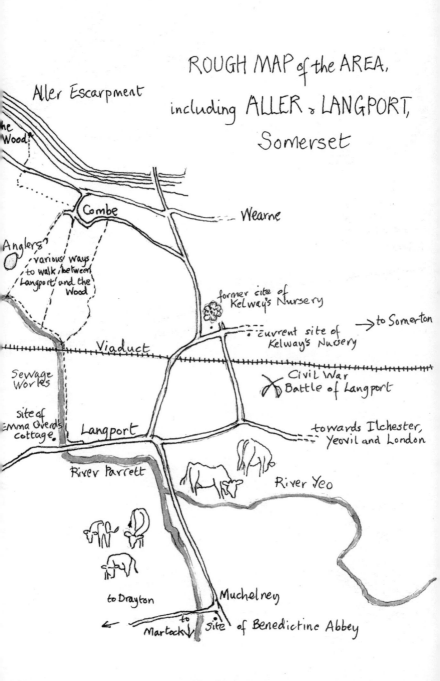

ROUGH MAP of the AREA,
including ALLER & LANGPORT,
Somerset

Aller Escarpment

the Wood?

Combe

Wearne

Anglers?

various ways
to walk between
Langport and the
Wood

former site of
Kelway's Nursery

to Somerton

current site of
Kelway's Nursery

Viaduct

Sewage
Works

Civil War
Battle of Langport

site of
Emma Overd's
cottage

Langport

towards Ilchester,
Yeovil and London

River Parrett

River Yeo

to Drayton

Muchelney

to
Martock

site of Benedictine Abbey

Contents

Looking up into the
Hazelwood

CHAPTER I

Searching for the Place

Generations pass while some tree stands . . .

SIR THOMAS BROWNE, *URN BURIAL*

I N THE LATE 1990S I was often on the road from London
to Bridgwater. I was born in south Somerset, my grandmother had lived further west, my brother was settled
in Bath. Family reasons were drawing me back to the West
Country, but this time the route led across a landscape I had
never seen before, of willow, water, grass, cattle, swans, ditches,
distant hills . . . the Somerset Levels. With their soft, painterly
light, spacious skies and melancholy, their feeling of not quite
belonging in the present, or at least of the past still being present, I fell for them.

Until then I had heard of the Somerset Levels without
knowing what they were. For a while in the 1970s they had
featured in the national news, in a controversy between farmers,
who wanted further drainage, and conservationists, who wanted
to save remaining wetlands. More recently, because of the
winter floods of 2014, the Somerset Levels again floated into the

national consciousness; but in general, neither expecting nor receiving much attention, they persist in their half-dreaming, vegetative way, a silted place of slow waters, eels, reeds, drainage engineers, buttercups, church towers, quiet.

Centuries of effort have gone into wresting pastureland from the once-wild marsh, then to combatting the ceaseless accumulation of sludge in the drainage channels. To have known the Levels as nature intended (in this, least ancient, phase of her intentions) would have meant living a very long time ago . . . as a Celtic saint rowing a coracle to a mound above flood level, a Saxon king in hiding from the Danes, a resilient marsh-dweller.

With the once-vast winter lake gone it would be easy to say that the landscape has changed beyond recognition, but perhaps not quite. The skies are still wide, the distant hills, Mendips, Quantocks, Poldens, Blackdowns, still give blue lines of definition between land and sky. The ambling rivers, however straightened, continue to make their muddy ways towards the Bristol Channel. Winter floods can create expanses of water astonishing to human eyes but instantly accepted by the swans, as though it were only yesterday that the floods were there every year. All this was new to me. What pleasure there is in learning another landscape, and the stories that have grown from it.

Not all at once, but over several journeys I felt the quickening of an old, recurrent wish: to plant trees. It is hard to say where this wish comes from. The desire to cultivate and make a mark is strong in my family, with plenty of gardeners, farmers, teachers, soldiers and a couple of missionaries in the few generations we can remember. But we have little continuity of place. Some people know that they are treading the same ground as their forebears, but we have moved about the globe too much for that. To me the very rootedness of trees is part of the attraction of growing them. That, and their longevity.

There is a lot of hope involved in planting a tree. First, that the sapling will grow at all, then that you will live long enough to see it becoming a real tree. But beyond that stretch years, perhaps even centuries, for the tree to go on growing and living, till people with no idea who planted it will love that old tree for its beauty, girth, the roughness of its fissured trunk, its long endurance. None of this is sure, especially with the erratic climate and the coming of new tree diseases. It can only be a matter of taking enough care, and hope.

Starting trees from seed is easy. Oak, sycamore, walnut, ash – they all spring up wherever they get the chance. I first began with tree seedlings in the 1980s but then had trouble finding permanent places for them. I suggested to my London borough council that we could plant up some fenced waste-land with trees, allow some growing time, then open it as a Millennium Wood. But *going green* had not yet been pressed upon local government. The somewhat baffled reply was that they had already put some interesting trees on a big round-about, so that was enough. The wasteland remained as it was for about a decade, with sycamores crowding up behind corrugated iron. When it was at last developed as expensive housing I realized how naïve I had been, not even enquiring about its ownership.

Over time and wasted seasons, it also became clear that planting trees on rented land, for instance an allotment or a caravan site, is too precarious. It is not good to see young healthy saplings, once a nut or berry or an acorn in your hand, cut to the ground. So to pursue this tree-planting idea it seemed that I, long settled in London, had to become a country landowner.

I had looked for land nearer home but not been able to afford it, so coming across the Somerset Levels revived my hopes. Their workaday modesty suggested that this might not yet be a land of expensive pony paddocks, that it might be the place to try.

The local land agents are Greenslade Taylor Hunt. Unlike the Levels, they were not quite new to me. Mrs Taylor, widow of the Taylor remembered in the current firm's name, had lived in Yeovil. As a child I had once tagged along with my father to visit her. She lived in a house built of soft ochre-coloured Ham stone, quarried nearby, with a big garden. In it we would see, said my father, a magnificent tulip tree. We did indeed see a magnificent tree, with leaves of a particular fresh green, but no tulips. Nor did I ask about them, my father being more given to statement than explanation. But still, I have noticed tulip trees ever since, with their odd-shaped leaves and their very occasional, greeny-yellow flowers (that can, at a pinch, be called tulip-like). It is a tree I would like to grow.

Greenslade Taylor Hunt has an office in Langport, an old town on the River Parrett. At that stage, however, the town was not my concern; it was land that I was after. I gathered that the idea of a piece of land having an asking price was too simple. It was more a matter of placing a bid in a sealed envelope, or of attending an auction. At my first attempt, after much cogitation, I failed to seal a large enough bid in the brown envelope. The six acres of ploughland above a railway cutting, where old iron markers saying GWR still lolled at the overgrown boundary, and in which I had been projecting a bosky paradise, soon passed out of my ken.

For several months afterwards, agent's details in hand, I would leave the main road back to London to go searching. Looking at fields is not like house-hunting, at least not in my experience. Perhaps if it is a large, valuable piece the land agent is an eager escort, but I never looked at more than six acres and was left to myself, with directions and the dread words 'You can't miss it'. It was winter, so it was often in failing light that I would at last discover which lane, which postbox, which gate I could not possibly miss, and see the 'FOR SALE' board poking through a hedge.

I am not a good forward planner, and had not prepared myself with the right points to look for: ease of access, availability of water, aspect, existing structures, apparent fertility, all of which I now know are important. I just relied on feeling. One site was unnerving, an old airfield with gaunt brick buildings and such a fell atmosphere that I had to jump in the car and reverse out quickly, crunching a rear light in the process. That was exceptional. Most of the places felt all right, but not seductive. Falling in love with places is not so different from falling in love with people but, again in my experience, is more reliable in the long term.

One field I saw was a warning. Someone had planted quite a number of trees but was, for reasons unknown, giving up. The trees were no more than saplings, planted close. Already, brambles and thistles were massing together, with the saplings just keeping their heads clear. The impression of struggle and dereliction this made was very far from the poem of graceful groves and waving grass I had in mind. I took note. It would not work just to plant trees, flit back to London and sit tight. Young trees need care.

Something else about that particular visit shook me, more than everyday worries about brambles. All the other sale details had led to places around Langport, but that field lay further south, between Yeovil and Crewkerne. As I approached, the names on signposts began to sing out. Without having at all prepared myself I was travelling back forty years, visiting memories of my father.

We had not stayed in Somerset after I was born, but the name had always been surrounded by a golden haze. Somerset was the place we had been happy. Berkshire, Hampshire, Surrey, Kent, wherever our fragmenting present happened to be situated, could not compare with Somerset. This was the general drift of my father's influence, the notion that to live in Somerset was best, other countryside good, suburbia bad, London anathema. Summer visits to my grandmother's house on the edge of Exmoor, surrounded by beauty and the scent of honeysuckle, seemed to confirm his bias.

My father had been wounded at Gallipoli in the First World War. Although physically he recovered well, in spirit he had more trouble. Lacking other options, after the war he stayed on in the Army, until delayed shock seems to have caught up with him. The older members of the family kept this so quiet that we later ones only caught the vaguest hints of a serious breakdown. He lived through whatever it was, and then, to the delight of his own family and consternation of my mother's, became engaged when he was over forty.

My parents met each other through one of my father's sisters. No one appears to have doubted the love between them, but what worried my maternal grandfather about this proposed son-in-law was his joblessness. As for so many men damaged by war, it was hard for my father to put a career together, especially when the Depression set in. There were also shades of difference between the families. My mother's people were teetotallers and Congregationalists. Any drinking was to them a Bad Sign, as may also have been my father's Church of England background and his Tory leanings.

Having left farming a generation or so before, my mother's family were in business, selling clocks and jewellery. My grandfather was not rich, but comfortable enough to feel dubious of a penniless suitor. Only on the stipulation that my father should find employment did he approve the marriage.

I heard about this many years later, from my mother's older sister, who had never had much time for my father. Between the lines of her story it was easy to read that, to her mind, the marriage had brought trouble to her sister. Indeed, although my aunt, a widow, had been happily married herself, her general view of men was that most of them were more trouble than they were worth.

Still, my parents loved each other. And they loved their three children, of whom I am the youngest. How we would all have gone on as a family is unknown, because my mother died in 1954, leaving my father heartbroken.

No one, including himself, seems to have thought that my father would have been able to bring up three children. My brothers were already at boarding school; I went to live with our aunt, our mother's sister. The ground beneath our feet was shaking, but we did not have to be told to keep a stiff upper lip. That was a matter of course.

After a few years, my father came to think that if he returned to Somerset things might get better. When he did so in the late 1950s he still knew people locally, so it was not unreasonable for him to hope that he was coming home. He bought a cottage in a village near Yeovil and tried, with only mixed success, to pick up threads. But while his confidence in old friends waned, his love of the countryside remained strong. Views, sunsets, fine buildings, trees always excited him. There is a huge tree, a redwood called Holy Tree, standing on its own at a crossroads near Norton sub Hamdon. It used to bring forth from him a cry of delighted greeting.

That day in 1998, seeking a field, I suddenly recognized Holy Tree again. It took my breath away. There it was, big, splendid, a great bear of a tree, and there it still is. Yet I was glad that the nearby field with the ill-grown saplings did not appeal to me. The names and the sights in that neighbourhood, iridescent with love and sadness, belong to another time in my life. It felt right to be looking for land in a county that had meaning for me, but in another part of it.

These were winter visits and yielded nothing to my purpose. But in the early spring of the following year I did see two different, much more beckoning pieces of land. One was described as 'three most attractive enclosures', the other as 'principally scrub, of interest to conservationists'. They were to be sold at the same auction. That use of the word *enclosures* was intriguing; surely it must be centuries since they were enclosed, why not just call them fields? But the agent was a man of few words, to me anyway, so I did not try to detain him on the subject.

I saw the attractive enclosures on a mild morning. It was quiet, with nothing but the sound of sheep and lambs' voices, and open views across the Levels to the Polden Hills. Birds rose up from the scoop of water which the sale details called a natural pond, a pheasant seemed to be nesting among the violets under a hedge. The lanes to this distant spot were, where they passed farms, muddier than any I had seen for decades. Such a sprucing-up of the countryside has been going on, it was exciting to see all that mud.

Robin, my farming cousin, later looked at the land for me. He thought it rather wet but did not doubt that trees would grow there. He said that a farmer would not give more than £10,000, but that you never know at auctions, anything can happen. I loved that place, with its feeling of being off the earth. I did all the right things – solicitors' searches and so forth.

The other piece of land, the scrubland that the agents had faintly praised as being of interest to conservationists, I saw in the last glow of a sunny spring evening. It was hard to find a way in. A rough grass track sloped up between a wheat field and an old orchard. The track ended where there must have been an entrance to the land I had come to see, but all was overgrown with elder, brambles and nettles. Trees were visible further up, but scrub was an aptly vague description of the muddle in front of me. The agent had advised that it was easier to get in higher up, so I carried on beside the wheat field to its top hedge. As the plan showed this to be the highest point of the scrubland, I climbed in over a ditch and a line of rusty barbed wire.

The footsteps of animals had kept open a thread of path, ushering me into a kind of wrecked wonderland. After quite an interval of further clambering, of holding back sprays of bramble or stepping over fallen wood, it was possible to take some unimpeded steps, thanks to huge hazels outgrown from coppice, in whose shade little else could grow. The evening light reached in, gilding the brown hazel leaves on the ground. Something half hidden by them turned out to be a skull with canine teeth. Lower down, two trees were leaning out beyond the shade of the hazels, their mossy trunks low to the ground but with life still in their dark, tangled twigs. Apple trees . . . so had this been an orchard once? They looked as though they belonged in an Arthur Rackham illustration.

Enchanted as I was by this place, there was one drawback: noise from the road. People say that it is easy to get used to the sound of traffic, but I disagree. Because of it I did not ask for solicitors' searches for the scrubland, but pinned my hopes on the quiet of the other fields, the three most attractive enclosures.

∾

The auction for both these properties was to be held in Langport on 20 April 1999. Knowing I would be bad at bidding, I asked the agent to recommend someone to do it for me. Without hesitation he said that Charles Fleming, a solicitor, loved auctions and would be just right. I also asked my friend Margaret to accompany me. Margaret and I used to teach together. When she retired she took on an allotment and more or less lived there ever after. From a no-nonsense background in Iowa, she was old enough to be my mother, very practical and shrewd, the perfect companion for this venture.

The main item of interest at the auction was a small farmhouse with nine acres of land. The four acres of scrubland belonged to it, but were being sold as a separate lot. I had been enjoying mild fantasies about that farmhouse. It was billed as needing complete renovation, but in my mind that translated into a coat of interior whitewash. I imagined being able to stay there in the summer. The thought that most work with trees needs to be done in the winter had not yet occurred to me.

On the morning of the auction, Margaret and I left London at 7 a.m. and drove through the rain to Langport. The event was to be held in the Langport Arms Hotel, but not till the afternoon, so we had the morning for looking around. We picked up the key to the farmhouse, just in case it was irresistible.

As we arrived in the rain, all looked damp and forlorn. The garden was overgrown, with paths beaten by potential buyers, or burglars, to both front windows and round the back. Inside we saw that the fireplace had been ripped out; stolen, we guessed, which turned out to be true. Stone flags indoors, steep wooden stairs, almost a ladder with hand grips to pull up by, apple loft running behind the bedrooms. No electricity, water from a pump, no kitchen to speak of, a privy outside with uneven stone steps but a roll of paper still in place. The orchard as in Sleeping Beauty, but the view obscured by the rain. Perhaps the bad weather was a blessing: if it had been a bright day I might have been tempted. Not that I had the money, nor was I thinking of leaving London. However, some things you just have to check, in case life means you to do a somersault. But on that grey morning the farmhouse felt mournful, as though all the spirit had drained out of it. No somersault was required.

On to 'my' fields. It kept on raining and raining, so the attractive enclosures were not looking their beguiling best when Margaret saw them. We only walked around a bit. It was strange leaving, not knowing if I would own them later that day. It was so wet we did not bother to look at the scrubland. In the auction schedule it was due to be sold before the fields, so we would not be bidding for it anyway. We had lunch in a pub instead.

The ballroom of the Langport Arms turned out to be more like a village hall, with dingy pink floral wallpaper. It offended Margaret more than me, I was too preoccupied. There was a bar at the back but only a few drinkers. The place was full, with at least a hundred people. Charles, the solicitor, said there were some local developers there, after the farmhouse. I was trying to guess who would be after my fields.

Contrary to the printed order, the auctioneer announced that the fields would be the first item of sale. This was a surprise and I could sense Charles revving himself up as the auctioneer sprang into his description. Charles had told me he would only join the bidding when he guessed it was above halfway; I had told him not to go above £15,000. The auctioneer was in high spirits, he too clearly loved an auction, but what he said in praise of the fields I was too nervous to hear.

The bidding started at £12,000. It rose so swiftly that we never got a look in before it sold for £19,500 without Charles having so much as twitched. This, when my cousin had said that no farmer would pay more than £10,000. The buyer was someone of the same surname as the seller. There was a feeling of excited anticipation in the ballroom: £19,500 was an unexpectedly good price. Charles, Margaret and I exchanged looks, but the charged atmosphere was too buoyant to allow disappointment to set in. The main attraction, the farmhouse, was next.

The auctioneer prefaced the bidding for the farmhouse with a word about the owners, Mr and Mrs Scriven. We heard that they had lived there till well into their nineties, but now frail health had obliged them to move, unlike Mr Scriven's father, who had lived there till he died, aged ninety-eight. The auctioneer was eloquent about the old-world charms of the property. Even though the fireplace and outdoor pump had been stolen, we were not to worry about the bread oven door: here it was, declared he, taking it from some sacking and flourishing it aloft. He rattled on about a sitting tenant, a wren nesting in the privy. Thus warmed up, the bidding at last got started, soon rising above the guide price of £70,000. The room was too crowded to see who was batting prices back and forth, but within minutes someone had bought the farmhouse for £116,000.

Next came the four acres of scrub woodland, the lot I had seen on a sunny spring evening but discounted because of the traffic noise. A lull had seeped into the ballroom, now that the main prize was gone. For weeks I had given no more thought to the scrub woodland, but now that the order of sale had been reversed and my desired fields were already lost, suddenly, here was a new possibility. I cannot remember at which moment this awareness broke in on me, but there was no time for a measured conversation with Charles about it.

Perhaps the auctioneer had not been thinking much of the scrub woodland either, because beyond dropping in the words *amenity* and *conservation* and noting that the owner of the lower orchard required the successful bidder to clear some fallen willows, he had little to say about it. The bidding had already got off to a slow start when I began nudging Charles . . . go up to £4,000, don't go at all, yes, no . . . but then things seemed to falter at about £2,000 so I thought, go on, isn't it a pity to leave with nothing? Charles, meanwhile, without any outward sign of attending to me at all, was quite equal to the occasion. Whether he winked or raised an eyebrow or a forefinger I never saw, but within a few more moments the winning bid for the scrub woodland was mine, at £2,750. I was to become the owner of a small piece of land, even though it was not the one I had chosen.

Grinning, dazed, I listened as though from a distance to the auctioneer discoursing on Moor Right, the arcane regulations of the grazing that formed the last part of the auction. It was perhaps a reflection of the bad times farmers were going through with mad cow disease that it did not reach its reserve.

I was to write a cheque for 10 per cent of my bid. As I gave it to the agent he said, expansively for him, 'your own little bit of England'. I was surprised. Patriotism, if that is what he was suggesting, had not formed part of my thoughts on this venture. But perhaps he had divined my motivation better than I had myself. Plenty of English people were at that time buying up land in France, Italy or further afield in Eastern Europe, but that had never occurred to me. As if by default, I had chosen Somerset.

Still being attached to the idea of the fields I had not managed to win, I asked the agent if he thought the buyer would part with the furthest (prettiest) one. Very unlikely, he said. So it was goodbye to my quiet fields. Later, when I heard more about the remote area they were in, and how it was no coincidence that the buyer and seller shared a surname, that nearly everyone around there shared a surname, I came to appreciate how unwelcome an intruder I might have been.

Whether I thanked Charles with as much warmth as I now feel he deserved I cannot recall, but it was with the feeling of making the most of the glass half full that I left the Langport Arms. Knowing that I was no longer going to be starting a plantation from scratch but adapting to an overgrown one, I set off with Margaret to see My Wood.

It was still raining. Great clods of clay attached themselves to our boots as we struggled up the ploughed field at the end of the grassy track. Nettles at the edge had grown enormously so we did not try to go in, just peered. It looked very dense, very wet but very beautifully green. The field maples were coming into delicate bronzy leaf in the outgrown hedge, which really is no hedge at all but just the line where the field stops and the scrub begins.

Further along the hedgerow, under a hazel we saw spent cartridges, some lords-and-ladies with pale, shapely spathes and a dark-green-leaved iris. By standing on tiptoe at the top of the track we could glimpse nettles and reeds clustering round the huge fallen willows that the auctioneer had mentioned. Brambles had made a smothering mound right over the trunks of the still-living trees and clumps of sedge were advancing down into the orchard. It was obvious that the owner was right: the willows were blocking the ditch. There was something comforting about having been told what was to be my first job, but I wondered if reinstating the ditch would mean that everything would then dry out. I was already getting keen on being the owner of a marsh.

Margaret was very encouraging. She liked the wood better than the fields, because of its being on a slope. Coming from Iowa, she said, makes one appreciate a slope, and she was not troubled by the sound of traffic. Though aware that Margaret was a little deaf, I drank in her words. We set off back to London, through the wet and increasing murk. About halfway Margaret asked me what I was thinking. I could only answer that I was just trying to get used to it all. 'I think you've been lucky,' she said. We got back to London without difficulty, although the rain kept up the entire day.

Chapter 2

Searching for the Genius

> . . . *all must be adapted to the Genius and Use of the*
> *Place, and the Beauties not forced into it, but resulting*
> *from it . . .*
>
> ALEXANDER POPE,
'OF THE USE OF RICHES'

HOW CHEERING is Alexander Pope's advice, in its confidence that any Place will have its Genius. My four tight-grown acres were sure to have one, or more than one, but to adapt to something you have to know what it is. Unlike the wealthy gentlemen Pope was addressing, eager to follow the fashion for landscaping, I was in no danger of letting loose a bevy of labourers to force beauties into the place. But one man equipped with power tools could come to much the same thing. Guessing the Genius of this Place would be shy, I started with secateurs.

The piece of land is an irregular shape, wider than it is deep, spread across the sunny slope between orchard below and rising ash wood above, a wheat field to the west and more ash wood to the east. It borders the land of three other owners, the farmer's wheat field, the lower orchard and the wood reaching down from a caravan site up on the ridge. The plan is clear enough, but the whole eastern part was so lost in thicket there was no guessing where the kinked line of that boundary lay. A ditch runs along part of the line between my land and the lower orchard, then turns down beside the track, taking a mixture of spring and rainwater across the moor to the River Parrett.

Having bought the land in April, I went in early May to meet the owner of the lower orchard, Mr Knight, to talk about the fallen willows. Here was proof that my friend Margaret was right when she said I had been lucky. A kinder neighbour than Ted, as Mr Knight later became known to me, would be hard to imagine. The land agent had told me that he was a farmer, but that was one generation out. His father had been a farmer, but when it came to the sons the farm had been too small to share, so his older brother had taken it on.

Ted, when I met him, was in the process of retiring from being a self-employed builder. But farming was in his blood, he said, and that was why he owned some fields, the orchard and a stable. Ted and his wife Doreen had brought up their son in the white cottage opposite the orchard, but later moved to a bungalow they built for themselves in the nearby village of Aller, where I went to visit them.

Doreen, wearing a Somerset Carers overall, served tea. 'You sounded so young on the phone, we didn't know what to expect, did we Ted?' said she, while he sat in an armchair, regarding me with courteous wonder.

Somerset was audible in their voices, but only mildly. It was nothing like as strong as I remember hearing among my grandmother's neighbours, whose conversation could have been in another language for all I could understand. No one now, to my hearing, still speaks such broad Somerset.

Although with Ted and Doreen there was no language difficulty, I did feel the need to sound plausible, or at any rate sane,
in trying to explain why I wanted the land. Skipping Alexander
Pope and the Genius of the Place, I made sure to mention about
having been born in Somerset, and that farming is in my blood
too. My mother and her older sister, the aunt who brought us up,
ran a small mixed farm near Guildford. This was in the 1920s
and 30s, when Surrey was still the countryside.

Having ushered in our new neighbourliness with tea, biscuits
and photographs of the grandson, it was time for Ted and me
to get to business. It was raining, but we set out to look at the
willows across the ditch. My farming cousin had said I should
establish who owned the ditch before undertaking any work.
According to Ted it was mine because it was up from the fence,
but as both fence and ditch were invisible under mounds of
brambles and the prone trunks, I had to take that on trust.
The willows were clearly mine. Ted said he had asked old Mr
Scriven, the previous owner, time and again to do something
about them but nothing ever came of it. I think we both knew
that I would be an easier touch.

Several things became clear during that conversation: that
Ted loved his orchard and was upset to see its top corner revert-
ing to marsh, that his son, Philip, was a digger driver and that
the son of a nearby farmer did contract work. We agreed that I
would see to the willows and brambles and then he and Philip
would see to the ditch. I was not sure my cousin would approve
this bargain, but it seemed fair to me. Ted led me further along
the top boundary of his orchard so that he could point out the
ash tree he said marked the division between my land and that
of the neighbouring caravan site. We peered up into the rising
tangle of boskage, overshadowed by ash trees, without seeing
any posts or fencing.

After we had returned through his orchard to his sheds, Ted introduced me to the two old ponies, Holly and Lucy. Comfortable-looking beasts, Holly was brown and white, Lucy was black, small and rounded. They had played a role in his son's courtship of the woman who was to become his wife, in that she had wanted a pony and he had been able to provide it with somewhere to live. Then another pony had been added, to keep the first company. But, Ted indicated drily, some time had passed since that successful sequence, and now much of their care had fallen to him.

There was never any haste in Ted's activities or conversation, but after a while he departed for lunch in his comfortable bungalow, leaving me free to push up into the dripping wood.

∾

Trampling, cutting, ducking, clambering, I got in at the top of the wheat field, crossed the relative clearing of the hazels and slithered up a slope where deer had left their slim, elegant prints and loops of old man's beard hung down like creepers in a jungle. The mound levelled off under another big hazel. Like a high window in the enfolding green, there was a tiny opening of view across to the opposite ridge a few miles away. It was only a glimpse of grey above a wash of grey-green treetops, but even on a wet day the sky was miraculously luminous.

In a trackless waste, I was beginning to realize, you need known points, places to recognize and return to. This mound with a view became one for me. I cleared an open patch there, cutting back enough undergrowth to make it A Place.

The rain had eased. I went down to the car to fetch some lunch, newspaper and matches. Picking dryish twigs along the way, I returned to the mound and started a fire. The damp made it slow, but after a while the flames gathered strength, giving out enough heat to set the steam rising from my coat. There was no shortage of sticks: everywhere around was cross-hatched with fallen branches.

It felt strange, that first meal on land I owned but that did not feel mine. The breeze was ruffling the leaves. Out of the corner of my eye I kept catching their movement and thinking that someone was about to push a branch aside and challenge my right to be there. There was a lot of birdsong. I felt the presence of the many unseen creatures for which this really was their place, the only place they had.

I was dishevelled and chill but it was all right, only a matter of starting moving again, with the comforts of a B&B in prospect. But it was striking how fast one does get into a muddy mess, and how hard it must be when living in the wild is not a game. A Bosnian woman had recently arrived with her seven-year-old daughter at the London school where I taught. Her story, coming to mind as I huddled up close to the fire, made my wood project seem an indulgence, like Marie Antoinette with her dairy.

It emerged that the Bosnian woman's daughter was really her niece, the child of her dead sister. Her own baby had been born, and then died, somewhere in the hills above her ravaged village, as she and her neighbours were fleeing the violence. Somehow, she and her niece had found themselves in Denmark, where a marriage had been arranged for her with a Moroccan man resident in London.

A while later the Bosnian aunt and niece departed as abruptly as they had come, off to another borough and another school. With so many people like them, rootless across the world, it seemed to me all the luckier that there was I, about to start planting trees in the county where I had been born.

It was time to hop about and loosen up. I wanted to cut a way through to the top of Ted's orchard, following the luminous patch of sky even though that was soon lost to view under the towering brambles. They were too much. After an hour or so, I had to divert the tunnel of hacked greenery back into a less dense area of tall, spindly trees.

There were a few apple trees here and there, decrepit but still alive and blossoming. The hollow, mossy trunk of one had opened out, making a curved interior like a wing armchair, an agreeable dining parlour for the fox, judging by the pile of red feathers on the dry ground inside. Within this living enclosure, which tipped forwards, the wood was ridged, dry and spidery. Above, it still managed to support two high trunks holding a canopy of leaves, blossom and mistletoe.

Already, when I first found that tree, there was a small split in the opened trunk, a squint window, through from the inside to the mossy exterior. As time went on, this squint was to widen more and more, making a deep gash, as the tree moved, shuddered, twisted towards its inevitable decline.

Further towards the margin with the wheat field, slim elms were struggling, but losing against Dutch elm disease. Many of the local hedgerows, I have since learnt, are of elm, and healthy if kept trim. Only when the hedge grows out into trees do the beetles move in under the bark and cause trouble, leaving tree skeletons to stand, a climbing frame for ivy, till at last they topple in the wind.

Next to the hazel wood I found one good, straight oak tree, sixty or seventy years old perhaps, and one less straight. Otherwise it was all ash, hawthorn, sloe, elder, field maple along the hedgerow, with big patches inside of the dark, spindly trees I had yet to identify. I now know them to be plum trees spring-ing up from underground rootstock, maybe the wild stock of once-cultivated varieties. Rotting branches lay haphazard on the ground, lords-and-ladies and hart's tongue fern flourished in one area, reed and sedge in another. As I tracked hither and yon trying to make sense of the maze-like space, it felt much bigger than it really is.

That first day in the wood I stayed till about 7.30 p.m. but was glad not to have brought a tent. Quite apart from the damp chill, the place felt secretive, mossy, withdrawn, intent on its own business. Happy to leave the animals to their own night-time devices, I walked down the track to the car, made some adjustments to hair and clothing and re-entered civilization.

The B&B hosts lived in a beautiful house in Muchelney Ham, not far from the ruined Muchelney Abbey. With its Ham stone, mullion windows and roses it was a picture-book house. The hosts were intrigued, very willing to gossip about the auction, the people involved, the prices. The woman talked winningly of 'a nice little field of ours called Egypt you could have had, quiet, lovely views', but then her husband added, 'Not for £2,750 though.' I took it all in, asking them what they knew of a nearby orchard that was coming up for sale. He could think of at least two locals who would want it: 'There's always interest in everything round here,' he said. I arranged with them that I could slip out of the back door early in the morning, go and listen to the dawn chorus in the wood and be back for breakfast.

Little by little over that first summer, I became more familiar with the place and how it came to be as it was. Mr Scriven had been scrupulous about keeping the deeds. The solicitor passed on a bundle of copperplate-written parchments and papers detailing at unreadable length the changes of ownership and deeds of title since 1793. There had been two adjoining orchards, Suggs Orchard, sometimes written Sugg's, and Long Hill Orchard. Given that they had been owned by the same family for most of the twentieth century, it was a surprise to learn that they had often changed hands in the nineteenth. Many of the owners were local, but some had lived as far away as Bradford, Surbiton, Enfield, so I was not the first long-distance owner, nor was I the first woman. The consistent thing is that they were always called orchards, not woods. I wondered who the Sugg of Sugg's Orchard was.

I had not thought of being an orchard-owner, of growing fruit trees. Oak, beech, cedar, walnut were more in my mind, trees that could still be here in two hundred years' time. But there was no mistaking that the Genius of this Place was less pretentious, a good, everyday apple sprite, who would only be content if at least the lower reaches of the land still grew fruit. I did not abandon my hopes of noble trees, just tempered them, so that the four acres became shared between orchard and woodland.

Mr and Mrs Scriven had moved into a nearby care home. By appointment, I went to visit them in hopes of finding out more about Sugg's Orchard and Long Hill Orchard, the varieties of the apples perhaps, or the identity of Sugg.

Mrs Scriven was in bed, seemingly asleep, while Mr Scriven, a rangy, spare-looking man, sat in a chair. He was alert, cautious but well disposed. They were both in their nineties. After I had been shown to a chair, another old man wandered in with a hopeful smile and gaping pyjama bottoms. A clucking mother hen of a carer soon shooed him out. I started asking questions.

Mr Scriven was hard of hearing. He also spoke with a Somerset accent, in the softest of voices, through few teeth. It might have been sensible to have recorded him, but I had rejected that as too formal. Despite moments of mutual incomprehension the conversation trotted along well enough. Afterwards I wrote everything down, to the best of my memory and understanding.

Mr Scriven's parents had been farming in Aller, but in an area so prone to flooding that they moved to Plot Stream Farm. (Perhaps it was in their determination to get out of the wet that the farm acquired its current name of Higher Plot Farm.) In 1920, as the deeds tell, they bought the property I had come to ask about, 'all those pieces or parcels of orchard land . . . containing together four acres twelve perches or thereabouts,' for £345. Mr Scriven would have been about sixteen then. In his nineties he could not recall the varieties of any of the apple trees in Sugg's or Long Hill Orchard but thought they would all have been cider apples, put in at different times as the older ones fell.

By the 1950s the price for the apples was so low it was no longer worth maintaining them, and there was plenty else to see to, cattle, pigs, sheep, voles (foals?) . . . I kept listening, puzzled about those voles. Keeping them up there, continued Mr Scriven, was not much good because the fox kept getting them . . . aha . . . fowls. But what about fencing them in? 'We did, but he was too clever.' There followed particulars of the fox's wiles, spoken so softly that I could only guess at them, prompted by Beatrix Potter.

Ted had mentioned that there was a pond hidden somewhere in the undergrowth. I was hoping Mr Scriven would tell me where to look for it, but instead he described in tantalizing, semi-audible detail how he had dug it 'for the beasts' and built a retaining wall. Each spring, however, it had to be dug again because the beasts trod it in. At the time of listening I thought that the built wall was retaining the pond at the bottom, so it sounded odd that it got trodden in each year. But later I found that the wall holds the bank at the top, where the water trickles in, and that the place the cattle trod was lower down. There, I came to realize, Mr Scriven had made what amounted to a loose cobbled strand of numerous lumps of blue lias stone, so the cattle could stand and drink without sinking into the mud. It would have been that strand that needed annual refurbishment. Did he do all this digging and stone-laying by hand? I wish that question had occurred to me.

That spring water, said Mr Scriven, was so clear and pure that you could drink it. He had once been approached by a man who wanted to keep special fish that could only survive in very pure water. But nothing had come of this because, if I interpreted his hand gesture aright, he had not wanted anyone else busying themselves on his land. On the subject of the spring, all of a sudden Mrs Scriven came to life, rising up from her pillows to pronounce, 'It never ran dry.' So she had been listening . . . I hoped she might say more, but she soon sank back down again.

Mr Scriven talked about an owl always perching on the same tree. I mentioned the spent cartridges, asking if he had given anyone permission to shoot up there. He had not, nor could he clarify the position of the lost boundary, beyond saying that he had once allowed a path to be cut across a corner along there, and then regretted it. 'But I always kept the deeds because someone may need them,' he said, checking that they had indeed been handed on to me. No, he did not know who Sugg was.

He asked if it was true that his farmhouse was being converted into a sort of palace or country club? Wondering if someone had been pulling his leg, I assured him that it was not, that it looked just the same. I then asked him, realizing the hopeless inadequacy of the question as soon as it was half spoken, if he missed the farm. 'Miss it?' he replied, incredulous. 'Ha . . . miss it?' The pain in his voice brought the frowstiness of the care home, the constraint of sitting at a bedside, all too clearly before me. He had spent a lifetime working out of doors. His father had not had to go into a care home because the next generation was there living in the farmhouse with him, but for this Mr Scriven there was no next generation to carry on. I do not think Mr and Mrs Scriven had any children, but even if they had, they would surely not have continued with that tiny farm.

It was time to end the visit. I left them as I had found them, Mrs Scriven in bed, Mr Scriven upright in his chair, two people for whom the idea of leisure was probably quite alien. They had made a living from a farm of thirteen acres, not like hippies or romantic ruralists but as though that were still a normal thing to do in southern England, right up to the eve of the third millennium. Even if I had not learnt much about the wood, it felt as though I had brushed fingertips with an era that was in effect over by the end of the Second World War. That is, before I was born.

The millennium was coming up; I liked the idea of planting some trees to mark it. But that first year was more a time of feeling my way, getting some idea of what to do. There never was a master plan, the place seemed to lay itself out according to necessity: the need to deal with the fallen willows and clogged ditch, to have some sort of a base, to open a route round the marshy bit. Despite this haphazardry, however, I did have an underlying sense of what I was after. I wanted to open up enough room for trees that might live for centuries, while restoring some of the land to orchard. I also wanted to keep areas of wilderness for the creatures, so that we could share the space without too much mutual inconvenience. And I wanted it to be beautiful. Not immaculate, that was too much to hope for, but, in its own ragged, benign way, beautiful.

At first Long Hill Orchard remained lost beneath brambles; it was only Sugg's Orchard I approached. Who was Sugg, I still wondered? Soon I had invented him as a faithful Saxon, rewarded with land by King Alfred for his help in seeing off the Dane. You cannot spend long in this part of the country without hearing of King Alfred, *the illustrious Alfred*, King of Wessex. It was in Aller church, in the form of a photocopied leaflet, that I began to understand what an historic place I had happened upon.

St Andrew's Church, Aller, a stone building begun in the twelfth century, is too young to have been the setting for the momentous event associated with it. Nor is it certain whether the wooden Saxon church it replaced was already there, or was built to commemorate Aller's moment of glory, which happened in 878. The year 878 is hardly a date resounding down the centuries, unlike 1066, but then 878 was only a Saxon victory, a partial one, of no propaganda value to the later Norman conquerors.

Looking down from the track leading to the wood, Aller Church and Aller Court are plain to see. Sheltered by trees, they stand about a mile away on the shallowest of mounds, with nothing else around except low fields. On veiled, hazy days, of which there are many in this damp area, their outlines are less definite, making it seem as though it would only be a matter of narrowing the eyes, of concentrating hard enough, to see Alfred and a company of more than thirty men making their ceremonious way along to the church, or mound-soon-to-be-church.

However, when I stand on the track, haze or no haze, the busy little A372 does a good job of keeping the ghosts at bay. What with the Tesco lorries, the hauliers going to and from the slaughterhouse, the cars and the white vans, Alfred the Great and Guthrum the Dane do not spring easily before the mind's eye. Nevertheless, in the year 878 the 'illustrious Alfred . . . stamped immortality on this less conspicuous spot'. It happened like this, according to John Collinson, antiquarian, writing in 1791:

> That King, having at Ethandune, or Edington, sig-nally overthrown the Danish forces, reduced them to terms of peace, and engaged on his part to resign the kingdom of the East-Angles to such of their people as would embrace the Christian religion. In pursuance of this treaty, Godrun or Guthrum their leader came to Alre, the place we are now speaking of, being in the vicinity of Athelney, with thirty of his officers, to receive the rite of baptism, and King Alfred himself stood sponsor for him at the font, and gave the barbar-ian convert the name of Æthelstan. The Danes staid twelve days after at Alre with the King, and were then dismissed with large presents of money.

The Anglo-Saxon Chronicle says much the same, in fewer words. So, a considerable royal party, all gathering in little Aller, needing food and shelter for twelve days. The Chronicle has them completing the ceremonies in Wedmore, about twenty miles to the north, so perhaps it was in Wedmore that the food and bedding and shelter had to be found.

How are we to picture this, in what clothes should we dress them, how are they to travel? At least we know it was early summer, so presumably the winter floods were gone, the cattle back on the pasture, the tracks not yet overgrown. Are the men on horseback, the defeated Danes under guard? Who is carrying the stuff . . . there must be stuff, surely, if there is to be a grand baptism and feast?

The oddest thing to understand is why Alfred chose Aller to enact this deed. The baptism of the pagan Vikings sealed the moment when, unexpectedly, their invasion of England came to a temporary halt and they had to content themselves with only part of it, and Christianity. It sounds the sort of event to merit grander surroundings, Glastonbury Abbey perhaps, yet it happened at Aller, which must always have been 'a less conspicuous spot'. The fields are still wet now; in 878 the area was undrained, with the river winding through exactly as it pleased. Neither then nor since can it have been an imposing place.

Aller is about fifty miles from Edington, in Wiltshire, where the battle in which Alfred halted the Vikings' westward progress is thought to have taken place, so proximity to the battleground is not what commended Aller (although there is a Somerset Edington with a rival but discounted claim to be the battle site). But, as the Anglo-Saxon Chronicle noted, Aller is *near Athelney*, the place where Alfred did or did not burn the cakes. Historians have been dismissive of the peasant woman and her scolding, but that a fugitive king, holed up after Christmas in a marshy hide-out, brooding about the future of Christianity in England, should be too distracted to mind cakes seems no less likely than the rest of the story.

Athelney, another mound in the marshes, had become Alfred's retreat after Guthrum had driven him from his winter quarters in Chippenham the previous Twelfth Night. From quickly built fortifications Alfred is reputed to have set out on raids against the Vikings, causing them dismay before vanishing back into the marshes along paths known only to locals.

So fondly did he later think of Athelney that he founded a Benedictine abbey there. Why then did he not choose Athelney for the baptism? To quote the anonymous author of the Aller church leaflet, who writes like a military man, 'Alfred chose the isle of Aller for the ceremony, probably because he suspected the Danes of treachery and wanted a secure site and, no doubt, he was reluctant to show them Athelney.' Well, maybe. What with 'probably', 'no doubt' and the lack of evidence, we are free to doubt and wonder all we like.

My preferred fantasy is that, while there was no church at Athelney in 878, the one at Aller already existed and that Sugg, a fine hulk of a man with cloudy blue eyes and a dry humour, would kindly escort Alfred to it for solace, on the occasional dismal day of February or March 878, when Alfred's cause, including Christianity in England, seemed lost. I have to admit that my search among the gravestones in Aller churchyard yielded no Suggs, and that the quality of the land of Sugg's Orchard would not represent much of a gift from a grateful king. But still my Saxon Sugg, imaginary as he was, took up residence in my mind.

CHAPTER 3
The Rollalong

I will arise and go now, and go to Innisfree,
And a small cabin build there, of clay and wattles made:
Nine bean rows will I have there, a hive for the honey-bee,
And live alone in the bee-loud glade.

W. B. YEATS,
'THE LAKE ISLE OF INNISFREE'

L IVING ALONE in the bee-loud glade was not my wish, even though the wood did turn out to be loud with bees with the blossoming of the wild plum trees. The trees are so tall that it took a while to work out where the buzz was coming from, but then, looking up to follow the sound, I could just make out the bees looping in and out of the froth of white flowers, bright against the blue sky. It still did not make me want to live alone there, but even if not to live in, to have some sort of small cabin became more and more desirable.

Arriving without any door to open feels strange. At least there were living beings to greet, so I soon developed the habit of bringing carrots for Holly and Lucy, the two ponies in Ted's stable. They were sturdy old things, living out their retirement without many demands on their time, but restricted as to eating lush grass because of a disease called laminitis. They were sometimes out in the orchard, but more often penned in their yard, polishing the galvanized bars of the gate to a high shine with their rumps. I grew fond of them, and they were fond of carrots.

Back and forth from London, dipping in as time allowed, I visited throughout the summer of 1999. Only once did taking on the wood feel a sad and lonely project. It was a sunny June evening, but I was carrying a dark mood from another compartment of life. This gloom made the brambles and nettles seem overwhelming, but worse were the odd traces of human passage: baler twine, cartridges, a half-buried carrier bag, a torn pair of men's underpants. They seemed to whisper of sinister goings-on in a derelict, unwelcoming place.

It took until the end of the visit for the mood to lift, as I sat under a big ash tree on the bank above the neighbouring wheat field, eating a picnic. The view was soft and dreamy, the sun slipping towards the horizon, everything warm, comforting, calm. All of a sudden the wheat started moving, the individual stalks bowing to one side in a diagonal line towards the bank. A moment later, out trotted a young badger. Purposeful and busy, the badger began sniffing the roots of trees along the bank until it almost reached me. But with a quick look of surprise, back into the wheat it turned, setting up a waving line far into the field. Then the waving stopped. What was the badger doing, I wondered, deep there in that forest of wheat?

Restored to equilibrium, I was able to see more cheering things on the walk back down the track: wild honeysuckle in flower by the ditch, calves with their mothers looking the picture of contentment in Ted's orchard. I said goodbye to the ponies and left for London, confirmed in the thought that for the wood to be enjoyable two things were necessary: open views, and some sort of secure shelter, in short, a version of home.

There was no question, officially at least, of building anything. The woman at the planning department said that permission was needed even for a shed, and that the chances were they would say no. My farming cousin was unimpressed. He cited the example of a celebrated Somerset racehorse trainer, king of the flexible approach to planning, whose formula was *don't ask, take a risk, apply later if caught*. For all that the beauty of horse racing shines out in a cautious world, I continued to listen to less daring advice. Ted thought a shed would get broken into, my brother foresaw murder. I wondered if one would be safer in a tree-house than in a shed, but then thought how cold it would be to sleep up there in winter.

A chance conversation with a woman who was a parish councillor yielded a piece of advice. She said that all the nearby parish councils were much exercised about New Age travellers, or anyone else wanting to dwell in fields or woods, but that, nevertheless, structures on wheels were more acceptable than those without. She dismissed my suggestion that a shed was less ugly than a caravan. 'The planners won't agree with you,' she declared, 'and if you do sleep in a shed the one thing you can be sure of is that people will know, and someone will shop you.' Her husband softened her warning with, 'Although you think no one can see what you're up to, someone always notices. But be patient; I expect if you're patient you'll get what you want.'

Anyway, there were plenty of other things to see to. In July my brother and I hired a chainsaw to try cutting the fallen willows, in case we could manage without the contractor. We enjoyed ourselves and so, it seemed, did the cattle in Ted's orchard. They crowded round the open car to watch as Martin dressed up in the elaborate safety costume, only backing off at the noise of the saw. But however nasty it sounded, the saw was not powerful enough to cut the thick, sappy trunks and could only manage the slimmer branches. By the end of the afternoon we had filled the car boot with logs, but looking back at the whole task, a lone mouse in a granary would have made more impact. It was time to ask Andrew David, the contractor Ted had recommended.

Andrew came to see the willows on a July evening. He reckoned there was about three days' work there for him and two men. He talked about machinery, including an advanced-sounding form of mower called a Jungle Buster with which he would approach my side of the ditch. This clearance was so sure to be an assault on the place that I was glad that I was going to miss it.

Andrew was not just interested in the job, he wanted to see the wood. So we walked round the accessible bits, with him recognizing a pile of dry grass as badgers' bedding here, kicking a spent cartridge there, naming two different sorts of elm in the outgrown hedgerow. It was clear that he felt on home ground. He said he had grown up just along the ridge in the village of Wearne, where his grandfather and father had a farm. But he sounded disappointed, dismissive about the farm. There was no future in it to provide for a young family, that was why he had his own business as a landscape contractor.

I asked how safe he thought a shed would be, tucked away out of sight. The local countryside, hitherto so placid in my estimation, began to bristle as Andrew replied; deer poachers, stock rustlers, machinery and metal thieves, siphoners of diesel sprang up from behind every hedge. Even with the pinch of salt I felt might be in order, it was discouraging. The contents of the imaginary shed, kettle and teapot, spade and secateurs, sleeping bag and bird books, would hardly please anyone who had taken the trouble to break in. The thought of a smashed-up shed was worse than that of no shed at all. Or suppose, even more alarming, that the shed did find favour and someone had moved in? I had to brace myself against such imaginings. After all, getting the wood was meant to be a joyful addition to life, not a source of gratuitous worry.

The husband of the parish councillor had recommended patience. I was not aware of following his advice, but in letting the matter of a shelter rest for the moment, I did in effect do so.

Even without a shelter, however, there was one item I needed straight away. A wheelbarrow, in which to carry stuff up the track to the wood. Ted kept one inside his open-fronted shed, between the small grey Ferguson tractor and piles of rusting metal rods. He let me use it but, although it was still in one piece, to ask his barrow to keep going up and down that overgrown track was like putting an old nag in for the Grand National. We agreed that I would get a new one and store it in his shed, for our shared use.

To buy a wheelbarrow sounds simple but is in fact, as I was surprised to learn, no such thing. In the past I had been aware of thinking well of wheelbarrows, of finding them modest, useful, attractive things, but was soon led to realize that mine had been a generalized, even flippant view. The new millennium was imminent, but there were still courteous men dressed in traditional brown overalls in charge of wheelbarrow sales in Langport, Somerton, Bridgwater, from whom I learnt that there is much to consider when making such a purchase. There are the questions of weight, capacity, material, construction, balance, type of wheel, durability, purpose, price. After extensive research I ended up buying a green metal barrow with inflatable wheels.

Wild Plum Blossom

The track in those early days was a world of its own, a never-mown strip between the wheat field and Ted's orchard, with the hedge and ditch running down one side. In summer its grasses, rushes and burdock grew above head height, becoming the sort of insect reserve a city park would herald with educational notice boards. The barrow, with its one wheel in front, was a good shape for pushing up through this tangle, a sort of prow cleaving the waves.

At the end of the voyage I would turn the barrow upside down to allow the scores of little insects that had fallen in to scuttle out again. It was a strenuous method of reaching the wood, and the later mowing of the track makes it easier to get up there. But I do regret the passing of all those little crawling and flying beasts, including grasshoppers, butterflies, moths, bees. I miss, too, the sense of being a submariner in a grey-green sea.

∾

Sometime later Andrew said that the clearance of the willows was done, but that it did look rather blitzed. It had been much more work than expected: they had found a dozen huge trunks folded on top of each other before they got down to the ditch at the bottom of the pile. We agreed to meet there with Ted and his son Philip to discuss the renovation of the ditch.

I arrived early, to have a private view. It did indeed look blitzed. A mashed emptiness was to be expected; it was the charred trunks of the still-upright willow stools and fence posts, the now-exposed barbed wire of the old fencing that gave it its desolate battlefield air. Pompeian heaps of ash stood at the top of Ted's orchard, big logs were stacked among the flattened reeds on my side of the ditch. There was a new scoop of space to look, even to walk into, before meeting a wall of elder. Wide but not very deep, this new territory was shorn and trampled, but at least it was open. I picked my way across the marshy ground, treading on a litter of broken twigs, leaves and reeds. Still dancing out from its background of dogwood and bramble the honeysuckle had survived, even though it grew close to the charred stumps. The ditch was a mass of blackened debris, with two plastic bottles floating in it.

The men arrived. We spent a fair time shifting from foot to foot, looking, speculating. The talk was of mini-diggers and JCBs. After a while it appeared that Andrew had torched the willow stools to try to return the ditch to a straight line. Burnt timber still blocked the run of the ditch, but he demonstrated with a kick that most of it was rotten, except the remains of the biggest tree. This blackened hulk was a pitiful sight, the rusty barbed-wire fencing that had become absorbed into its trunk kinking out in twisted gestures on either side. Although it looked dead, 'Soon green up, he will' was the general view. No one thought it was worth the effort of uprooting the trunk – better to accept a curve in the ditch. The discussion turned to the springs that feed the ditch; how far up the ridge did they rise?

I had been on the lookout for these springs. There is no mains water nearer than the ponies' stable, so for tree-planting it would be good to find a natural source. My cousin had given detailed, if puzzling, instructions on how to tap a spring, but the first step was to find one. In early August I had been elated to come across a hand-basin-sized hollow, mud-sided but full of clear, cold water above the trickle leading down to the ditch. Convinced this was a spring, I pointed it out, but Andrew said that it was only a break in a drainpipe. Drainpipe? Ted confirmed that there were runs of clay drainage pipes all across the slope, put in long ago to improve the land. As we stood looking at the sludgy ground he added, 'Well, it *is* called Sugg's Orchard.' I asked what he meant, wasn't Sugg a name? 'No,' said he, pointing towards the messy squelch, 'that's zug.' As in soggy? 'Yes, zug.'

Ted was not to know that in that short dismissive syllable he was banishing my Sugg, fondly imagined aid to King Alfred, to non-existence. I half wanted to engage with him about the occasional apostrophe in the deeds, making it Sugg's, and about that final *s*: how, had there been a bog, the name might have been Boggy, not Boggs Orchard. But Ted's tone had been simple, incontrovertible, as though naming things for a learner of English . . . that's a flower, that's grass, that's zug . . . no room for quibbling.

I was loath to abandon Sugg, but he and King Alfred were not the only characters I had been co-opting into the story of my patch. William Pitt the Elder, Earl of Chatham, had appeared on the horizon.

To be precise, it was not Pitt himself but the very top of a monument he built that had been catching my eye on the horizon of the opposite escarpment. So little of it shows above the distant trees that sometimes it seems to be there and sometimes not, but a trip to the Taunton side of the village of Curry Rivel proved it was not an illusion. There, across the fields, rises an elegant cylindrical stone column ornamented with what looks like a dovecot with an urn on top. Way to the left is the hint of a big house behind trees, with a few cedars straggling in between. There was no information at the roadside, but a nearby farmhouse offered B&B. In mid-August 1999 I booked in for a night.

Staying in a B&B has its awkward side. The hosts have to appear to welcome strangers when really it is the money they most welcome, the guests have to tiptoe about, trying not to derange the dried flowers or plumbing, then look grateful at breakfast. On this occasion there were no other guests. Descending in the morning from my large, sparse bedroom, I found myself seated at the head of a huge Victorian dining table. There was an extensive family tree on the wall but round the table only a family of empty chairs.

Trying to ignore the atmosphere of absence, I partook of a ceremonial boiled egg. My host, scion of the extensive family and server of the egg, seemed no more relaxed about these arrangements than I was, but was helpful about the monument, The Burton Pynsent Monument. He pointed out names on the family tree that had some bearing on its story, and brought a photocopied article from *Country Life*, September 1987, entitled 'Appealing Pillar of State' – appealing because at that time funds were being sought to stop the monument from falling down.

These funds must have been forthcoming, as my host offered to arrange for me to visit the monument. Delighted at the prospect, I started reading the article. What a different world opened up . . . in recent times a brown envelope stuffed with cash or even a duck-house can get a politician into trouble, but here was William Pitt accepting from Sir William Pynsent, sometime MP for Taunton but whom he did not know, the promise of a whole estate, offered for no apparent reason.

As it happens, the bequest seems to have been more quix-otic than corrupt. People did soon suggest a link between Pitt accepting the estate and his opposition to a Cider Tax. But although William Pynsent, like any Somerset farmer, might have been outraged by the tax, he was too old to benefit in person from its repeal. In 1763 Sir William was not far from his own death when the last of his children died. His wife was already dead, his other potential heirs seem to have displeased him. In a big old house with only a housekeeper and servants for company, it is easy to imagine him fretting about who should inherit. He admired Pitt for his patriotism. That seems to have been reason enough to choose him. His only expressed hope was that Pitt would like the place well enough to live there when not in London.

Pitt, an enthusiastic landscape gardener who moved among people used to inheriting estates, accepted his good luck with éclat. According to Horace Walpole, old Sir William did not cease to fret even after his will was written, but set his wandering mind to think of other possible heirs, Wilkes perhaps, or General Conway. Pitt was lucky to have been named and even luckier that his name was still in the will when Sir William died in 1765.

In the spare, foxed quiet of the B&B dining room the crunching of toast and clatter of tea cup on saucer sounded brash, but the comforts of reading saw me through. When it was time to go I caught a glimpse of children's paintings on the kitchen wall, but where were the children? The best hope was that they were on holiday, that they would be coming back. It was the sort of house that needed children.

Taking leave of my host, I followed his directions to the farmer who held the key to the monument, down a sharp, steep lane. It is a feature of these escarpments rising above the Levels that, although not really high, they feel it. The approach to the farmhouse is dignified by a run of red-brick Tuscan columns supporting a barn, just the thing to please an eighteenth-century politician playing at rural life. The farmer gave me the key, pointing out the way up to the monument.

Pitt is said to have set about landscaping his new inheritance with speed and energy, causing shrubbery walks, a flower garden, hothouses, avenues of trees, a wilderness, lawns, all the usual requirements of gentlemanly gardening, to spring into being. So fervent was he, perhaps manic, that darkness did not stop him: he had the men out planting cedars by lamplight, exhausting the stock of all the tree suppliers for counties around. The designs were his own except for the monument, for which he employed Capability Brown. But by the time I walked up across rough fields and into the shade of a wooded slope there was little of all this to be seen, only the remains of the cedar avenue and the four-leaf-clover-shaped plot of grass on which the monument stands.

Sheep were lying at their ease on the steps to the plinth of the monument as I approached and looked for the door. Let into one of the four stone sides, it was made of steel with two padlocked bolts protected by an overhanging flange. The flange got in the way of opening the top bolt, a drift of dryish sheep droppings encroached the lower. With the droppings as a kneeler, I struggled with the stiff padlocks and bolts, wondering whatever I was doing there.

Once inside, daylight showed the start of a spiral staircase leading up into gloom. There was a cool, stony smell. Assailed by fantasies of locked towers, I pocketed the padlocks before starting to climb. The thought that, padlocked or not, the bolts would be unshiftable from the inside struck me at about the fifth shadowy step, but without enough conviction to force a retreat. Just as it seemed the whole climb would be in darkness, a blur of beckoning daylight came reaching down. The excitement of the building, the perfect placing of the window slits so that there was always just enough light to make out the steps, were so pleasing that they banished anxiety . . . I was not Rapunzel, after all, or a rebellious Chinese concubine. The steps, each dipped in the middle, led up and up.

A flood of daylight announced the last twist of the spiral. I stepped into an airy stone chamber with windows looking in all four directions, open except for mesh grilles. These apertures give the monument its dovecot look from far away. The views across the low-lying farmland to north and west stretched and stretched into the hazy distance, ending in rows of hills, Poldens, Quantocks, Blackdowns, with the Wellington Monument sticking up like a pencil. Much closer, almost as though you could lob a ball into it across the river and the railway, was my bit of wood, easy to recognize because of the big wheat field next door. It made sense that it was visible from here, since it was from the wood that I had first seen the tip of the monument. It seemed to put William Pitt and me into waving distance. Although I could not respond by raising a monument, not least because my land does not go up to the ridge, the idea of planting cedars in my highest corner, echoing his, began to form in my mind. I looked for another landmark, the War Memorial on Ham Hill, but rainclouds shortened the views to south and east.

Comforting daylight came looming up the last few of the 170 downward steps, the steel door was open, the sheep calmly in place as before. They roused themselves for a token scattering as I locked up and looked at the initials carved into the stone. The official inscription is *Sacred to the Memory of Sir William Pynsent Hoc saltem fungat inani munere*. Even with the help of a dictionary later I could not get the Latin to make sense, but my sister-in-law says it means something like *May this monument at least furnish a trifling gift*. But it was more than a trifling (inane) gift. Who would remember Sir William Pynsent now, but for this handsome tribute?

Well, I have since come to the surmise that, memorial or no memorial, Sir William is still remembered, but with resentment. When the B&B host was pointing out his family tree he said rather more than I could take in, but reconstructing it in the light of things I have read since, it seems that the estate Sir William Pynsent willed to Pitt was only his by marriage. His late wife's family contested the will, but lost. How galling it must have been to them to watch the mercurial Pitt wing in, spend money like water on a new house and landscaped garden, then lose interest in the place and disappear. It is unlikely that it was any consolation to them that Pitt's children and grandchildren enjoyed the freedom of their holidays there, but I love to think of the young Lady Hester Stanhope riding about on that ridge with the far-reaching views, building up, perhaps, the wanderlust that turned her into such a bold and distant traveller.

Among the unofficial carved initials on the plinth to the memorial, many with nineteenth-century dates and written in dignified Roman letters, a scratched recent one stood out, saying, 'Eclipse, 11/8/99'. Clouds permitting, it would have been a good place to have watched the eclipse, grander than the bare French field from which I happened to see it, with a hare dashing across and the automatic lights of a battery poultry house blinking on as the sun was dimmed.

With his energy, brilliance, self-confidence William Pitt would have knocked my patch of land into shape in no time. As well as running the country, or perhaps in one of those intervals when he was not called upon or was too ill to do so, he would have had the spring tapped, built a hermitage, opened up vistas, replanted the orchards. It would all have been done fast, with no worries about planning permission or thought of expense, even though his pockets were not of the deepest. There again, he might have retired to his invalid's couch and suffered, at the same time as leading everyone else a dance. I admire that bravura approach to life, without at all being able to emulate it. Six months after the auction at which I had acquired my wood, three months on from identifying as imperative the need for a secure base, I had still not even solved the question, what sort of base? Then, easy as winking, it was solved for me.

At first I had no idea what Ted was talking about when he announced, 'I was going to put the Rollalong in the Western, but then I thought of you.' I kept quiet, waiting for clues. 'The Western' was easy. The *Western Gazette* is the local newspaper, whose headlines read exactly as they did when my father used to take it: 'Yeovil Man Gaoled', 'Ilminster Bus Driver Fined', 'Fury over Wasps' Nest'; but what was the Rollalong?

It turned out that I had passed the Rollalong many times. It stood outside the ponies' stable, a grey sealed metal cuboid that I had registered as a container. Like the big locked shed across the yard from the stable, it was something to do with Ted's building business. I liked the pitted sign leaning against the corrugated-iron wall of the shed, saying E. R. KNIGHT AND SON, BUILDERS, and the grey Ferguson tractor parked in the open-sided barn, but the Rollalong had never before attracted my attention.

A Rollalong, Ted explained, again as though to a learner of English, is a mobile site cabin. If I liked, we could look inside. He opened a door, brought out a two-step ladder from inside and fixed it below the door. I was ushered into a dim, mildewed interior. There was a window, currently covered by a metal shutter, a built-in table between two benches, a kitchen unit with sink and two-ring gas top, a wall-mounted gas fire, a rail for coats, two gas lights and a large sloping table top for spreading out builders' plans. One corner of the space was walled off with a separate door from outside. 'This is the toilet,' said Ted, opening the door to show a dead spider, a hook, a gas light and some empty space, 'chemical toilet that is, you'd have to put one in.'

To say that the Rollalong was heaven would be to exaggerate. It was dingy and smelt of damp, but for my purposes it looked perfect. There were wheels to please the planners, it was modest in size yet had most of what I needed, the metal shutter would make it more secure than a caravan.

I had once owned a caravan and knew to ask about rust on the chassis. The Rollalong stood on metal legs at each corner, its two wheels raised off the ground. As we peered underneath at what looked like quite a lot of rust and yellow peeling paint, Ted bashed here and there with a spanner, saying, 'He's not too bad.' Apart from flakes of yellow paint nothing fell down, and the clang of metal on metal sounded firm, so I took his word for it.

A surprising number of wires and pipes ran underneath. The pipes were for bottled gas, the wires for the rear lights when the cabin was being towed. The remains of a registration number can still be seen, scribbled on the back door. Ted had bought the Rollalong from Somerset County Council; it had been used by a gang of roadmen. He himself had not used it very much.

As soon as Ted mentioned roadmen, I imagined Bob Bart sitting engaged in some sort of deal at the Rollalong table, his cloth cap removed to reveal his sparse, flattened hair. Bob Bart was a timeless rogue who had lived along the lane from my father. Mr Bart's official job was as a roadman, but he had diversified. He cut all the local men's hair, including my father's, knew everyone's business and could procure any sort of goods. In my father's case this was only Dorset Blue Vinney cheese, then nearly extinct, but Mr Bart would handle it as though it were contraband, keeping his supply chain secret. He was a wiry, flinty man with bloodshot blue eyes, a gamekeeper's son. His old mother still lived at the edge of a wood in a cottage so damp and sunken that the parlour windows were at ground level. She shared it with her grandson, another gamekeeper.

A big elm stood across from Mrs Bart's cottage, its lower branches hung with carcases of rooks, squirrels, magpies, rats, all the gamekeeper's enemies, some freshly dead, some withered, hanging so low a walker had to duck. These macabre arrangements were still current in the early 1970s. Bob Bart may have been a rogue, but not very lovable. Mentally I evicted him from the Rollalong table that was not yet mine.

Ted said that he had been going to advertise the Rollalong in the *Western* for £600. As soon as I agreed to pay his asking price it was clear he was surprised. Realizing I should have haggled, I tried to recoup lost honour by throwing in a proviso about the locks and that the gas fittings should work. We talked about the desirability of painting the outside green, so it would be less visible among the trees than with its current dull silver. He agreed to fix the locks, a bar to bolt the window shutter from the inside, and the gas fittings, and that the cabin would be towed up the track. I was to do the painting before the move, in order to make use of the water supply and the trestles Ted kept in his lock-up. Looking back on these arrangements, it seems as though Ted must have been expecting a fair bit less than £600, but was kind enough to make up for my deficiencies as a negotiator.

Towards the end of October I stayed a night in the pub in Aller. Gypsies had been at it again, I heard at breakfast, setting fire to a hay barn in reprisal for the farmer foiling their robbery of the village pottery. Gypsies, I was beginning to gather, were assumed to be behind every theft in the district. Whether they were traditional ones, New Age travellers, or indeed existed at all was left vague. For all my metropolitan liberalism and sympathies, I liked the thought of that iron bar Ted had added to the defences of the Rollalong.

Painting the Rollalong with green bitumastic paint, standing on a trestle in the warm October sun was a pleasure, especially as Ted's view was that there was no need to do any preparation. The name 'Rollalong' appears in bold blue bubble writing on a white ground on both sides of the cabin. In the interests of camouflage perhaps it should have been covered in green paint. But, with its echoes of the open road, it is such a cheery name that I left it, although aware that this particular wagon may not roll again.

Having wiped the mottled mould off the ceiling and scoured and scrubbed, I painted the interior white. Insects emerged from under loose folds of the vinyl on the floor, got themselves stuck in the paint and had to be squashed. It was surprising how much blood they had. I pondered whether it was their own or that of others. Either way, their winter hideaway was at an end.

To light the gas fittings was not straightforward. Ted was leery of gas, not being used to working with it. He checked the pipes, connected the cylinder and stood looking nervous in front of the two rings of the cooker. After what seemed a long time and a quantity of spent matches he remembered there was another tap to turn . . . the little blue flames popped up, catching round the bigger ring till it was all alight and definitely working. The smaller ring lit too, and even the grill, despite being bent and crusty. It was a moment of triumph.

The triumph did not extend to the lamps or the fire. The lamps needed mantles, the fire made noises as though it wanted to catch, but could not do so. Soon after that the term *thermo-couple* entered my vocabulary, but knowing the name of what you want and getting hold of it are not the same thing. Finding the gas mantles was easier. I studied the packaging, hoping for instructions. They were *Made in Malta*, they were *Not Radioactive*. Comforting as this was, it did not help with the question of how to fit or light them. Gas mantles, it soon became clear, are very fragile. Not wanting to wreck all of them, I gave up for the moment and returned to London.

The very next morning, standing at the back of the Wigmore Hall, I became aware that, as well as music, I was hearing a quiet roar. If I had had a seat the roar would have been inaudible, but as it happened I was leaning against the panelling at the back, just below – I craned to look – yes, it was a gas lamp. Never before had I noticed that some of the lighting of the Wigmore Hall comes from gas lamps, yet here was this timely, serendipitous discovery. After the concert the floor manager, a courtly old gentleman, demonstrated the delicacy required to light a gas mantle.

∾

Rollalong Moving Day was set for Monday, 20 December 1999. I had chosen a site beyond the marsh, tucked behind a curtain of willow. It was near enough to Ted's orchard to have the hint of a view but not so open as to be obvious from the road. After much debate about how to avoid sinking the cabin into the marsh on the way in, and some improbable suggestions involving the sort of temporary bridges used by the Army, we had decided that Andrew should cut an inverted horseshoe swathe through the trees, to keep the route on firmer ground, and make a clearing for the cabin. To my relief, this new 'drive' looked good. Opening up the site in a pleasing way it represented, it might sound impressive to say, a successful design decision. In fact it was an accident born of necessity.

Another lucky thing was the weather. The ground was very wet but a sharp frost had firmed it up. Andrew had arranged for a local farmer to bring his tractor. I arrived from London to find the party assembling near the stable, Ted, Andrew, the farmer and his collie, Max. I was unsure why, but we loaded some filthy paving stones on to my nice clean Rollalong floor. They hitched the Rollalong to the tractor and set off up the frosty track, Max capering about and looking as though he would get under the wheels. Ted stayed behind, conversing in his usual gentle, circular style, while I itched to be following the cabin with a camera. Progress up the track was slow, so I caught up at the top.

The entrance to my land has a particularly wet side but the frosted ruts held and the vehicles took it in style, only pausing where the slope is sharper for Andrew to rake bark chippings across the way. By the time they had rounded the top of the horseshoe and were trundling down into the clearing, it became obvious that the Rollalong was going to wind up facing the wrong way, that is, with the window giving on to the wood instead of the view.

Getting it turned round was not the work of a moment. It involved discussion, the felling of more trees and putting a rope round others to work as a winch. It did not appear to be going well. I was already cold from a long drive without a working car heater, so left the scene to fetch a thermos. By the time I returned the men had succeeded (I was never sure how) and were placing the paving slabs under the metal legs at each corner of the cabin. The farmer, Max and the tractor departed, Andrew fixed up the gas cylinder and went to fetch a spirit level.

Alone in my new shelter, I turned on all the gas rings and stood trying to catch the updraught of warm air, it having proved impossible to get the fire mended (no gas fitter will want to come out to a cabin, I had been told, and if he did he'd probably condemn the lot). A hint of warmth began to steal upon me as I drank coffee and waited. If not cosy, it was still a joyful interlude. Sneaking in just before the millennium turned, I had a wood and somewhere to nest in it. I would not see in the new year there, but the land would be waiting, ready to take on a new phase of its long life in the year 2000.

When Andrew had finished his adjustments we locked up and left, not without, on my part, some concerns for the Rollalong's safety. There was just time in the short day to pick mistletoe and get on the road to London, past flooded, frosty fields, partridges fluffed up as round as rabbits, lapwings flying over the moor.

The Hillock above
Ted's Sheds

CHAPTER 4

Rollalong Days . . . and Nights

My heart dwells here,
In rotten hut on weeping clay;
Tends here her useful herbs, her bloom;
. . .
Stockdove in oak,
Stormcock in elder, finch in thorn,
The blackbird in the quicken, jay,
Starling that spoke
Under the roof before the day,
. . .
All these are laid
Safe up in me, and I will keep
My dwelling thus though it be gone:
My store is not in gold, but made
Of toil and sleep
And wonder walking all alone . . .

RUTH PITTER,
'THE LOST HERMITAGE'

L ONG BEFORE spending my first night in the Rollalong, back in the 1970s I heard Ruth Pitter speaking on the radio. According to my memory she spoke of living in a hut in the woods, alone but for the surrounding birds and animals, and her calling as a poet. She sounded a free spirit. The difficulties of being old and isolated she dismissed with, 'The situation is untenable, of course, but I don't worry.' Without meaning to, I stored up her words.

Or thought I had. Between my remembered version of the broadcast and the facts that I have been able to trace, there is a discrepancy. It seems that as a child Ruth Pitter loved family holidays in a dilapidated woodland cottage in Essex, but that later she lived with a friend, surrounded by a large garden, in the village of Long Crendon. She was only alone after the friend died. The 'lost hermitage' sounds like the Essex cottage, only without the family; the Long Crendon garden could be where she tended her useful herbs and blooms, but not while living in a hut in the woods.

Anyway, at the time of my first Rollalong night I was still encouraged by the belief that a woman much older than me had lived alone in woods and been blithe about it. But I was not up to her airy dismissal of risk, thanks to another hut-in-the-woods tale, this one salted away since childhood.

My brothers and I had been to the cinema. After the main film came a second one in which Edgar Lustgarten took down a file from a shelf and introduced the re-enactment and investigation of a murder. An old man had been playing the violin in his shack in the woods. The unheard murderer approached from behind and coshed him with a plaster cast, of Beethoven perhaps, causing his blood to run along the floor and down between the boards. The complacent narrator demonstrated all this, the proof being the dried blood he revealed by lifting a floorboard. There were other bits I cannot retell, having had my eyes shut.

Once the film was over, how restorative it was to get out of the cinema and into the ordinary Croydon street. We all went home feeling cheerful. But by bedtime I was wide awake with fright. Our aunt's house was outside Croydon and edged by woodland, full, as it now seemed to me, of murderers. She scolded my brothers for having let me watch something so unsuitable. They protested their innocence: how were we to know?

For weeks I lay awake at night, seeing murderers in every moving shadow, fearing their approach through windows or up drainpipes. When I had first moved to live with our aunt, the cries of screech owls used to frighten me. Now murderers had joined the party. Also at that time the bedroom walls seemed to buckle, pushed from behind by murderers, although I have since wondered whether that might have been the onset of astigmatism rather than a case for Edgar Lustgarten, or indeed Dr Freud. My murderer panic took a long time to subside. I never told anyone about it. In my childhood we adhered to the maxim *least said soonest mended*.

Although decades had passed since then, I was struck by the thought that here was I, preparing to spend nights alone in a wood, just like the murder victim. Not just like. I would have a mobile, I would not play the violin, I would lock the door. This time it was my brothers who were the more worried. We had met that afternoon in connection with the decline of the last, longest-lived of our many aunts.

This aunt was not the one who had brought us up, but the youngest of my father's sisters. According to him, she had been sweet-tempered until the Second World War. She was good-looking and, so it was said, wore her Army uniform with style. But then, as my father speculated, there had been an unhappy love affair and she had turned sharp. Sharp is certainly how I, as a child, perceived her. In old age she had become touching, confused, irascible, a vulnerable relic from a world in which it was normal to trust a stranger at the front door.

It was the ninety-eighth, and last, year of our aunt's life, during which she could no longer live in her own home. For some years before having to move, she had been making lists and labelling things to be handed on to us and our cousins, then changing her mind, crossing out, reallocating. I had seen my name attached to candlesticks, then a clock, then a print, none of which were there later on. A lot went missing because, as we imagined it, she had not wanted to admit to conmen that she did not recognize them, and had handed over whatever they claimed to be collecting for repair.

Once when I arrived I had been surprised to find a policeman keeping my aunt company, a fact for which she could not, or would not, account. He explained that she had allowed herself to be taken to the bank by a man with a ponytail and earring, in order to withdraw the £5,000 she had agreed to give him. The teller knew that it would be an event for her to withdraw £500, let alone £5,000, at which hiccup in his plan the ponytail and earring had vanished away.

For all that, there was still a fair jumble of her possessions left after we had had to move our aunt into a home, which my brothers and I had been sorting before we parted outside her emptying flat. It was to be my first night in the Rollalong, so I hurried away, hoping to arrive while there was still some light left in the short February day.

Visible from some distance, a storm cloud was hanging over Langport, but there was only a hint of rain as I unloaded stuff into the wheelbarrow by the ponies' stable. It was darkish by the time I started bobbing up the track, carrying all manner of supposed necessaries, some of them just gleaned from our aunt's abandoned kitchen. I lit the candles in the Rollalong and set off for a load of bedding and cushions. A half-moon came out, glinting on the marsh. The third trip was in light rain.

Propping a torch on the hitch at the back of the Rollalong, I fixed up the gas bottle to the metal pipe that dangles out from underneath, tried the connector to see it was firm, and felt pleased. To have got that right meant having light and the gas rings working. But it did not mean heat. The Rollalong's wall-mounted fire remained unmendable so, on a previous visit, a Dalek-like heater with its own tucked-in gas bottle had made the journey up in the wheelbarrow, and now awaited its debut. I was fairly sure I could get it to light, having once done so before, but it still felt good when, after some hesitation, a rosy tinge began to spread across its chalk-white face. Then, with due care, I lit the gas mantles.

Having sat for a self-congratulatory moment, I disliked the pale, staring effect of the gas lights and turned them off, sticking to candlelight. My aunt's fluted teapot and the silvery thermos flask she always had on her tea tray twinkled in their new positions on the laminated surface beside the gas rings. It was time to warm the soup, pour some wine and feel at home. The only trouble was that there was still a very long February evening, then night, then early morning stretching ahead. I was not only wary of outsiders, but also about health and safety. With the metal shutter down no one could intrude, but then there would be no way out if there was a fire between me and the door.

I spoke to my brother on the phone. He was agitated about ventilation, thinking I would nod off with the gas fire on. I chose not to mention the means-of-escape question, but discussed the desirability of having a blackout curtain, to be able to keep the shutter up but avoid advertising my presence with a glowing window. It is surprising, as I had observed from the track, from how far away the glow of candlelight can be seen. In the course of a rather Gothic conversation I sought to reassure him, and myself, by saying I would sleep with a hammer to hand.

Actually, the only trouble in the night was cold. Despite layers of carpet, lilo and double blanket underneath, then sleeping bag, eiderdown and, after a while, coat on top, it was still cold. The old habit of wearing nightcaps began to make sense. I wound a scarf round my head and wondered, however do people manage to sleep rough? There was the sound of deer trumpeting, far off, and rain on the roof. All in all, I loved it.

The next day was beautiful, warm enough to sit out and read, perched on a bench of logs made just about comfortable with cushions and coat. The wood seemed to be fizzing, clicking, tingling, something anyway, tiny clicky sounds. Wondering if it might be the water trickling its underground way down to the ditch, I tried putting my ear to the earth in good Girl Guide fashion, but a sting from a nettle sprout put a stop to that. There came a sound of wingbeats but only a glimpse of two birds flying over, not big enough to be swans . . . small geese, large ducks? I planted roots of lily of the valley opposite the Rollalong door, taken from plants with a decades-long family connection.

Before returning to London, I called in on my aunt in her new care home. She was still surrounded by a number of her own things, prominent among them the toy animals that had come to mean a surprising amount to her. She seemed resigned to what had happened. Thinking she might like to hear about her fluted teapot, her bread board and so on, I tried to tell her of their rehoming, but curtains of deafness and memory loss hung between us. News of teapots in Rollalongs in woods was only adding to the confusion, so we reverted to how I would, yes I really would, give a home to her toy animals when the time came. And so I have. The bears, ducks and rabbits that came to share her second childhood and which, so she told my brother, sometimes danced in the branches of a tree outside her care-home window, slumber on in my attic.

Apart from the cold, and the long hours of winter darkness, I was happy sleeping in the Rollalong. I could just about fit under the plan table but found it was better to sleep half in, half out into the narrow gangway, with candle, matches, mobile and hammer ready on a corner of the bench. Another of my aunt's possessions that came up in the wheelbarrow was a chamber pot, so there was no need to go out in the middle of the night. But it was sometimes magical to do so, to happen upon the stars blazing above the circle of tall, dark plum trees and feel a sort of intense aliveness all around.

The nights were not silent: there might be owl hoots, dog barks from the kennels on the ridge, rain on the roof, a car passing along the road below, the deer's rough voices, an occasional scuffle or cry, but mostly it was quiet quiet quiet. I had a battery-powered radio but found I did not want it on much, in part because of the need to keep a fraction of an ear out for murderers, but mainly because real quiet is absorbing, it makes you want to listen to it.

The Rollalong is small inside, designed as a daytime shelter for workmen, not as a place to sleep. The fittings are all inbuilt so there is no moving things about to make more room for sleepers. As a consequence, only the hardiest have been Rollalong guests, of whom I most admire Margaret, the friend who accompanied me to the auction at which I bought the wood. Well into her seventies, she made no complaints about sleeping on a lilo near the door at an angle occasioned by the scarce floor space. It was more important to her, she said, to be able to get out easily than to be parallel with the wall. Perhaps it was a good Feng-shui alignment because she claimed to have slept well.

In other, handier, hands the Rollalong might soon have been transformed into a snug, insulated nest, bunk beds in place of the plan table, wood-burning stove with proper chimney, all the delights of the new versions of a shepherd's hut. But my project was to plant trees; I was trying not to get sidetracked into home improvements.

Summer nights were easier. Sitting out in the clearing, a fire in the terracotta chimenea, citrus candles against the midges, odd rustlings and peeps from birds here and there. Alone or with friends, those evenings were a joy. In the end it was the length of winter nights and the cold that drove me to the distraction of buying a ruin of a cottage in nearby Langport.

Langport, although smaller than many villages, is a proper town. When I first went there in search of a land agent, I warmed to its worn, unpretentious look, its haphazard mixture of old red brick and grey or ochre stone, of Georgian, Victorian and more recent buildings. It was down at heel, and to judge from this entry in a Somerset guidebook of 1907, had been so for a while: 'Langport, an unattractive little place, but it has seen some history.'

The cottage I was offered looked as though it had seen some history too. It was a wreck, but still occupied by an old widower, who slept downstairs in the only space the rain had not yet penetrated. A variety of musical instruments, including two pianos and a harmonium, mouldered in the damp, cluttered rooms, from the walls of which water-stained 1960s papers fell in scrolling folds. The cottage is right on the main street, but a very long, thin garden leads down to the open moor at the back. When I first saw it, this garden was half filled by a runaway leylandii hedge. It was time that the old man, as his children wished, should move into sheltered housing and that I, as everyone connected to me thought, should stop sleeping in the wood. The London house was easy to remortgage so I became what I had never foreseen: a second-home-owner.

Getting the cottage refurbished took time, but all, by and large, went well and now the cottage is more comfortable than the Rollalong ever could be. But that does not mean my allegiance has altogether shifted. The Rollalong remains the nerve-centre of everything I do in the wood, the place where the teas and coffees are made, the wine poured, the tools, books, outdoor chairs and binoculars live, the retreat when it rains. A new curved roof, put on to stop leaks but also to soften its boxy appearance, and a later coat of grey-green paint have taken it two steps in the direction of the desirable shepherd's hut, but no further.

∾

Once they knew I had a wood, friends, and friends of friends, started giving me sapling trees in pots . . . sweet chestnut, horse chestnut, oak, walnut, rowan, beech, ash, birch, field maple, hawthorn, hornbeam, hazel, yew, wild cherry, all the common lovely trees that seed so easily and long to grow, but have chosen a spot inconvenient to their neighbouring humans. No one offered me sycamore. Sycamores are like pigeons, too common for their own good. When sycamore seedlings sprang up in my aunt's woodland garden near Croydon we pulled them up, while those we missed grew into gangly, spotty misfits in dark corners.

It was not until I saw a full-grown sycamore in the middle of a courtyard in Provence, its wide reach casting generous shade, that I realized what a fine tree it can be. I feel wistful about that tree, but although my London garden is always offering sycamore seedlings, I have never taken one to the wood. This is because there are none growing there already. I have enough trouble trying to control things as they are, without adding another plant that loves to multiply. But if all the ash trees were to die, and no equivalent disease has arrived to kill sycamore, that might well be the moment to welcome them.

Four acres sounds spacious, but when I started there was no open ground for planting. The curved track cut for the Rollalong's arrival let in some light, so I began to line that with some of the chestnuts and walnuts. It is no wide avenue, if they were all to flourish and become big trees the track would narrow to a path, but that was a distant problem. The immediate one was the group of potted trees with roots pushing out at the bottom.

I found that some of these seedlings, released from their pots and with their roots unwound, would need quite deep holes. Delving with the spade, then trowelling up clay, I was reminded of the sound you hear when making a globular coil pot out of clay. Nearing the neck, reaching in to smooth the inside sets up an echo, and here I was schlurping out clay with a trowel and hearing the same echo. To be planting trees in wet clay pots did not seem much better than keeping them in plastic ones, but I put in stones and compost at the bottom and hoped for the best.

Most of the saplings grew but the sweet chestnuts, one after another, started to sicken. For several years they clung on looking pitiful, their leaves pale, twisting, the veins lined with black, before giving up. But the walnuts did better. I was glad about that, having nursed a fondness for walnuts ever since a man I was also fond of, an American, rented a flat in a grand part of Kensington. At the back was a yard with garages, and overhanging the yard a tall, wonderful walnut tree. It was September when I first frequented that place and huge nuts were showering down, only to be swept up or crushed by cars. They were the most delicious walnuts I ever tasted.

My American went back to America. Thanks to him I later saw banks of *Cornus mas*, the cornelian cherry, lighting up with their early yellow blossom the hillsides below the Cloisters Museum in New York. That sight added another tree to the list of those I wanted to grow.

The Atlantic is wide, but that was not the only thing separating my American and me. Suffice it to say, there was soon a time of dwindling, but for more years than I went on seeing him I would return to the yard in Kensington to gather those under-appreciated walnuts, until the arrival of security gates put a stop to it.

That was not, however, before I had several of that tree's descendants, sprouting in pots. But where could they grow? Vine weevil grubs ate the roots of most of them but one is, against the rules, growing on part of an allotment in London. It bears plenty of nuts which the squirrels take while they are green, so they may or may not be as good as those from the parent tree in Kensington.

I watch that tree with concern, because it occupies the half of an allotment that I later had to relinquish. Some of the tree has already been cut away by a subsequent plot-holder; a new one might finish it off. This story bears directly upon my decision to buy land. Unless you own the land you are not free to grow things where you like, to make mistakes, to *spuddle about*, as my cousin puts it.

The walnuts I planted at the wood are not descendants of the Kensington tree, but of other London and Somerset trees. They are excellent, willing growers, but confronted by a more mischief-making race of squirrels than the London ones. These Somerset squirrels seem to delight in the taste of sap, walnut and horse-chestnut sap particularly. To satisfy this desire, they rip off great strips of soft bark in springtime, leaving stems with young leaves to droop and blacken into sinister-looking bundles. In the case of one horse chestnut, they gnawed away enough bark to kill the leading branches, leaving a criss-cross pattern of tooth marks on the bare wood. I assume it is squirrels, not tall deer or flying rabbits, although rabbits do climb the sloping trunks of old apple trees for a hungry gnaw in winter, leaving piles of droppings on the moss. The exposed flesh of the gnawed tree turns a strong burnt-orange colour, showing up against the mossy green.

On a woodland walk arranged by the Farming and Wildlife Advisory Group I learnt a new verb, 'to hopper'. We heard about squirrels and their increasing damage to young woodland, with prophesies of future woods of misshapen, stunted trees. The only answer, said our guide, was to hopper the squirrels. I go on these walks meaning to learn. But they are often in beautiful places, so as soon as the talk gets technical or takes a mechanical turn, which is usually very soon, my attention can wander.

In the case of hoppering the squirrels, I must have missed a sentence or two, then found myself picturing some tall device along the lines of a cherry-picker, and wondering why the squirrels would wait for it: surely they would be the ones to hop? 'Of course you need to keep filling them up' was an aside that did nothing to help. But at last it became clear: to hopper a squirrel is to hang cones of poisoned bait in the trees you wish to protect. There was no sign that anyone else in the group had qualms about this idea.

I admit, the ideal woodland squirrel would not strip bark, would share nuts with humans, would entertain with acrobatics rather than race off, but I prefer the less-than-ideal ones to be gnawing, scrabbling, squabbling than writhing from poison. Looked at in a rosy light, it is just about possible to see some of their toothwork as a form of pruning. The walnut trees have grown bushy under this regime, or stunted and misshapen, according to your outlook.

In the decade or so since that woodland walk the squirrel damage has worsened, making the necessary rosy light harder to summon. So the recent sight of a young chestnut with its bark stripped right to the ground was enough to propel me into attending a *squirrel management* day. I knew that the talk would be of killing, but maybe we would also hear of milder methods of control, the squirrel contraceptives mentioned in the press, for instance. Bracing myself, I drove to a west Somerset farmhouse, parking in the cobbled yard alongside muddy four-wheel drives.

We gathered in a meeting room, the older men in tweeds, the younger in fleeces. Of the very few women, one turned out to be so fiercely dismissive of 'the fluffy bunny brigade' that I felt glad not to have broken cover. Sure enough, within a moment of speaking the host made plain that *management* meant *death*.

Death, that is, of grey squirrels, those nasty incomers. Red ones, our native ones, are a different matter. They too strip bark, but that did not appear to count against them. They belong here. It was hard, with the frequent mention of Brexit, not to hear echoes in some of this.

The only thing that was really pleasing came in a quick aside: 'poisoning's gone'. Not, it seemed, because it was cruel but because it was ineffective. Instead, trapping and shooting are current, but contraception is a long way off. The man describing traps was an enthusiast, speaking of *bait stations* and *baffles* with gleeful intelligence. There followed a long and detailed survey of the different traps available, plus eagerly sought advice on the DIY construction thereof.

The subject moved on to pine martens and their possible reintroduction to southern Britain. These fine, sharp little creatures with big ears have a taste for squirrels. But it did not sound as though dropping off a pair of them in the wood would be the answer. So, feeling somewhat more overcome by being such an outsider than decisive about my bark-strippers, I meandered back over the Quantock Hills. The likelihood is, those squirrels will remain free to strip away to their heart's content. I would no sooner trap them than poison them. And pigs might fly before I ask Andrew to shoot them.

Squirrels you expect in a wood, but there was, for a while, a far more improbable visitor. Smallish, scruffy, very shy, the llama started appearing towards the end of 2000, becoming a celebrity along the ridge for a couple of years. He was always referred to as 'he' but the red-brown hair was so long I was never sure . . . was he quite small because he was young, or because he was female? He did not seem to be growing any bigger. Either way, he was wild. The rumour was that he had been kept with other llamas but, at some moment of transfer, had declined to get into the llama-carrier, absconded, and continued to decline all efforts at recapture.

There was a llama enclosure at the far end of the ridge, where the land drops down to Sedgemoor and the llamas could, maybe, fancy themselves at an Andean eminence. The rumour continued that our llama would, when he felt like it, go and talk to his kind through the wire. Otherwise, said Ted, he was friendly with the sheep and not at all friendly with the ponies. He was often in Ted's orchard. In winter Ted put out hay for him which he took, even coming quite close, but never too close.

Whenever I arrived the first thing I would look out for was the llama. Often as not there he would be with the sheep, up on what looks from there like a conical hill but is only the end of a subsection of the ridge. With a few conifers and an oak on top, it is a place of singular character. Add more height and it might be the sort of hill an Italian painter would choose for St Jerome and his lion, or to sketch in a glinting cavalcade as it twists its way down to the plain.

If the llama was in Ted's orchard when I arrived he would stop for a long look at me, then unhurriedly retreat from view. Sometimes I would find his droppings, shiny as beads, or tangles of long, red hair on the barbed wire. Only once did we come face to face, down from the hazel wood where, concealed by wild plum trees, I was removing weeds from round a walnut sapling. We stared at each other, but he must have been less pleased than I was. Without the frightened haste of a deer or rabbit, but with determination he brought the meeting to a close, trotting off and disappearing past the quince tree.

As far as I could gather, everyone liked the llama. I worried that he might be shot during the foot-and-mouth epidemic but he survived that by quite a while. Then, time after time when I visited, there was no sign of him. At length I heard that he had

The Stray Llama
standing in Ted's Orchard

been found dead under a hedge further along, cause of death unknown. I still miss him, and find myself looking up towards the hillock when I arrive, hoping to see him, to recapture the magic of his appearances. He was our own local unicorn.

In the early years of my time in the wood it was as though one creature after another would introduce itself for a brief meeting. 'I'm showing you I'm here but want as little as possible to do with you,' seemed to be the message. The young badger in the wheat field was like that, as was the one and only bullfinch I have ever seen there, and the mallard duck. So, too, were the slow-worm and the grass snake. The slow-worm was safe under a heap of branches, but I was glad not to have injured the grass snake as it hurried away through the thick herbage I was shearing. There are always woodpeckers about, mostly green but also spotted, and plenty of robins, blackbirds, tits and other small birds that I fail to identify. The cuckoo calls from some hidden reedy place across the moor, and sometimes I think I hear a nightingale, or hope that it is a nightingale.

Mice, voles and shrews must all be plentiful. They rarely let themselves be seen, but a mouse once stopped at my feet in a miniature clearing between buttercups, held captive by what looked like overwhelming surprise. From its pointy nose and whiskers right down its glossy back to its long tail and delicate white feet, it trembled. In my best coaxing tone I said it had nothing to fear from me, but that the buzzard was about. It trembled on as though spellbound. To break the spell I moved. In the twinkling between my lifting a foot and putting it down again, the mouse was gone, vanished under waves of buttercup leaves.

❧

As well as giving a rough chance to foundling trees, I bought saplings from tree nurseries. The wood has no address so it is easier to collect than to have goods sent, and more fun as well. I had admired a stand at the Chelsea Flower Show that looked like a miniature woodland for the airiest of sprites, full of feathery leaves of translucent greenish-yellows or soft reds, colours to lift the heart, like wine held up to the light. The nurseryman spoke with an accent to match, rarefied, patrician.

This calm, ethereal impression was both sustained and dashed by visiting the actual nursery on a windy day in June. On the ethereal side was the appearance of a tall, slight woman, seemingly blowing rather than walking into the village. Although it was dry she wore a long raincoat of faded red with matching hat. When my friend and I slowed to ask the way, the lady of the raincoat leant down, holding hat to head, and spoke in the same courteous, old-fashioned, gossamer way as the nurseryman. Yes, she did know where the nursery was as it was her husband's, no, she did not need a lift there.

This breezy prelude had not, however, prepared my friend or me for the fly-away scene that awaited us, with the nurseryman distractedly skittering about and mumbling, trying to stop potted trees from blowing over. 'It's been dry and now this wind, no one's been watering properly, sorry, so sorry, have you come far?' It was clear that our arrival was a nuisance but we were not to be put off. My friend was there to choose a tree for me, and that was that. 'From London,' she said, making it sound as though we had come direct.

Through flapping polytunnels, over spooling coils of hosepipe, up and down concrete steps that might once have given access to former greenhouses but were now just part of the general obstacle course, past breeze-block sheds with Crittall windows we progressed, all the while admiring a special oak from Mexico, a Chinese beech, maples from the Himalayas, weeping birches, creeping willows, fastigiate hornbeams. It was marvellous.

While under cover our guide could focus on his potential customers, but out in the wind he had to keep darting about, righting blown-over pots, muttering 'Very rare, very rare' under his breath. Despite this staccato approach, we arrived at a decision: a pretty copper beech with irregular pale-pink edging to its leaves, as though it had been dabbed with a fine paintbrush.

I did wonder at the time whether this beech might not be too choice for the conditions that would confront it, but the nurseryman knew the Aller escarpment and thought it might be all right there. Which for a while, it was. But why, out of the whole wide wood, did woolly aphids choose that particular, jewel-like beech tree to descend upon, sucking its sap and smothering the tender backs of its leaves in their nasty, sticky selves? I suppose because it was already weakening.

For two summers I washed the aphids off and the beech kept going, although not flourishing. But by the third spring only some of its buds opened. It was clear, as I trimmed off the dried ends of twigs, that it was fading out. Then the friend who gave it to me became ill. I did not at all think the two things connected, but it was still a sad coincidence. If she had asked how the beech was doing, which luckily she did not, I would have spun a tale of good health and vigour.

The weather was quite different when I next visited the tree nursery, on a still February day, clear and cold. I was after hollies, in particular one that would have yellow berries. To get a holly to have any berries at all takes some calculation. They are fastidious about pollination and will not make berries with just any old, dark, prickly character. The nurseryman invited me into the warmth of a caravan that looked, like the Rollalong, as though its travelling days might be over, while he checked the compatibility of my proposed varieties.

This took some time, long enough for me to appreciate the gold Chelsea Flower Show certificates propped above the books of reference, and peaceful enough for a robin to whirr in through the open door and alight next to the biscuit tin. With one elbow keeping his place and his eye still on the book, the nurseryman eased open the tin lid, speaking familiarly to the robin as he gave it crumbs. A good while later I left with four hollies, two birches and a cornelian cherry, the last to be planted in honour of that blossoming hillside below the Cloisters in New York.

The other tree nursery I visited was quite different. Tucked in near the M5, it is a workaday wholesale business, supplying the landscaping trade. I heard about it through the Farmers' Wildlife Advisory Group, which was why I was lucky enough to count as a wholesale customer. This nursery could not be further from the teashop and scented-merchandise end of the scale. When I sought advice about the heavy clay soil and making conditions better in the planting holes for the young trees, the response was robust: 'Don't try cossetting, just choose things you know are all right for clay and let them get on with it.'

My stricken realization was that I had not given much thought to whether my chosen trees were all right for clay, but had dwelt more on those I liked and how they would look. But it was late at that point to start dithering about the plants, some bare-rooted, some in containers, now assembling on the counter. So off I set with a mixture of ones I felt confident about, weeping willow, goat willow, aspen, native hedgerow plants, larch, and some that seemed doubtful, not to say pretentious: two cedars and a magnolia. They were all small and fitted into the car. If they were to be moved now, it would need a huge lorry.

∾

The willows were easy to place, because there was space down by the ditch and the marsh. In went the weeping willow, the goat willow, which I had been wrongly told is like pussy willow, and a corkscrew willow a friend's mother had grown. There is a good outlook across to the moor and the river from there, which mattered because of an effect I wanted to emulate. Speaking of a fiery stemmed pollarded willow, my farming cousin had exclaimed how in winter, when the stems are brightest, the scarlet-orange colour can be seen from miles across the valley.

I had taken several wands from that very tree, which, as all willows do, had rooted easily. I planted them right above the ditch, hoping that they, too, would one day burst forth from the winter greys and purples, lighting up the scene from a distance.

Another plant my cousin gave me was marsh marigold. Like the red of the willow, that bold chrome-yellow is a lift to the spirits. It flourishes in the damp soil because, luckily, the reinstatement of the ditch did not mean that the marsh has gone away. Some years the ground is marshier than others. In summer the land further up can bake and crack, but down towards the ditch it keeps to its true, watery nature.

∾

Water and ditches come into the story of both the battles for which the area is known, towards the end of the Civil War, and, forty years later, at the defeat of the Monmouth Rebellion.

It was halfway through 1645 before the Battle of Langport took place, by which time there does not seem to have been any local enthusiasm for the war. People were already tired of the struggle, not least of pillaging soldiers bringing poverty and disease.

The Parliamentarians had won at Naseby, releasing Sir Thomas Fairfax to turn his attentions to the South-West, an area of mixed loyalties but mainly Royalist control. One of his aims was to free Parliamentarian Taunton from siege. The Royalists, who had a small garrison at Langport, held the north Somerset seaports, through which they were hoping reinforcements would arrive from Wales. Lord George Goring's intention was to hold back the Parliamentarian advance until the reinforcements got through. The Battle of Langport, usually dismissed as a minor skirmish, was only meant to be a delaying action.

The fighting took place on 10 July, starting on the slightly higher ground east of Langport. It had been raining, so the stream now called Wagg Rhyne was full. The stream ran in between the Royalist soldiers drawn up on Ham Down and the Parliamentarians on the opposite slope. These are not hills, just gentle pastureland. Goring got there first, in time to set up two cannon and some musketeers by the ford.

To get at their fellow enemy, their friends' friends, their distant cousins, the men of the New Model Army under Sir Edward Massey had to pass the cannon and the musketeers to cross the ford. Opinions vary as to the exact site of the ford, but it is not easy to picture armies of men and horse anywhere along there. Now, at any rate, it all looks too small and cluttered, and contemporary accounts also speak of hedges in the way. But get through they did.

Two troops of Parliamentary cavalry charged across the ford and up Ham Down, breaking through the Royalist lines. More followed, there was fighting on horse and foot. Then there was panic. Royalists lucky enough still to be on horseback galloped away. Some went through the town, setting fires as they went; some rode across the moor with the Parliamentarians in pursuit.

Near Aller some of the Royalists turned to make a stand, as Joshua Sprigg, a chaplain to the New Model Army, recorded, 'in a plain green field (where the passage out was narrow) called Aller Drove, but received only a piece of a charge, and then seeing our bodies coming on orderly and fast, faced about and never stood after: the passes being narrow in many places and the ditches being wide . . . many horses were lost in the ditches . . . and the riders got into the meadows hoping to escape, but could not'.

Alas, alas. What a hideous, disfigured mess must have been left behind, where someone may have been hoping for a second hay crop. And what of the wounded, the dying, human and horse? Nothing, except for the remains of a young man buried at the top of Burrow Mump, who may have died in that battle, or later in the Monmouth Rebellion. There were reports of many wounded carried to Bridgwater. The victors, Oliver Cromwell, Thomas Fairfax, Edward Massey, stayed the night in Aller, as had King Alfred before them.

It is in the nature of these events that some men did get away. One account speaks of fugitive soldiers seeking shelter in the woods above Aller, in other words, on the escarpment where my wood lies. Did any of them run, or limp, through those four acres? I have heard that the odd bit of Civil War metalwork turns up along there. So far, I have only found the remains of a watering can.

It is also said that, on moonlit summer nights on the hill opposite Ham Down, you may hear the faint tramp of marching feet and the sound of soldiers, singing . . .

Forty years later, there was support in the West Country for the Protestant Duke of Monmouth's rebellion against his uncle, the Catholic King James II. The Duke was an illegitimate son of Charles II. Many people felt they had done better without a king, once Charles I was gone, and were not keen on kings, least of all a Catholic one. Bridgwater offered free quartering for the Duke of Monmouth's rebel army.

The rebels were hoping to spring a dawn attack on the king's army camped behind Westonzoyland, but chance, it seemed, undid them. It had to do with a ditch. In the early hours the horses' hooves were muffled for the approach from Bridgwater, but as the cavalry queued in the half-light to cross a temporary bridge over the ditch, off went an accidental musket shot. (Or was it deliberate sabotage? There are different versions.) With the surprise lost the battle was lost, and the Duke soon knew that things were hopeless. Abandoning his supporters, he fled south, hoping (but failing) to escape across the Channel. Plenty of local people, for whom his cause had seemed a stand against tyranny, were left to be rounded up and held in Westonzoyland Church, before being hanged or transported as convict labour to plantations in the West Indies. A Bridgwater woman spent the rest of her life in Antigua, for having sewn a rebel banner.

In the course of time and political change the convicts were pardoned, but most had no money for the sea passage. Very few got home.

First Tree, with all
The good apples out of reach

CHAPTER 5

Apples, and Other Early Encounters

Here's to thee, old apple tree,
Whence thou mayst bud
And whence thou mayst blow!
And whence thou mayst bear apples enow!

TRADITIONAL WASSAILING SONG

I T HAD BEEN fifty years since anyone had tended the apple trees in the wood. Of those left, some were only twisted trunks on the ground, the stumps of branches jutting out like horns, the insides rotting to a rich red-brown. Their lives were over but there was still a beauty in their slow, continuing disappearance. I tried to plot from their positions, and those of the ones still living, how the planting rows had run. But there were too many gaps and too much intervening growth.

As far as I could see, there were about seven apple trees left alive in the Sugg's Orchard part of the land, in varying stages of decline or entrapment. It was not until later that I could reach those in Long Hill Orchard. In Sugg's Orchard a tree was lying in a graceful attitude inside a dense tent of bramble, sending out a few slender twigs into the light. These twigs blossomed in 2000. Later on, I picked two foggy-looking apples from them. A tree so tenacious would surely respond well to more light and air. I was determined to set my Sleeping Beauty free.

It took days to do so. As rat-catchers say, *you have to respect a rat*, so I came to respect brambles. It is not just that they can climb up and over a small tree, spill down the other side, take root as soon as their tips touch the ground and then start all over again; it is the spread of their lateral stems, branching, branching, branching with thorns all along, holding on tight. Living bramble branches grow over an increasing mound of brittle, cinnamon-brown dead ones, with thorns dried all the sharper for lack of sap. They are hospitable to the robins nesting unscratched among them, but not to the human out to remove them.

A friend helped me finish off the bramble imprisoning the Sleeping Beauty. After two days we came away tousled and smelling of woodsmoke, wrists stinging, full of self-satisfaction. Partial self-satisfaction would have been more fitting. The tree I was so sure would love the kiss of new light and air reacted very differently, taking exposure so ill that within a few years it was dead. The only good that came out of all that work was incidental, a new passage open to the Rollalong.

Brambles were not the old trees' only warders. Ivy clung to some, others were so intergrown that it was hard to tell whether apple was leaning on elder or elder on apple. My favourite, the one with its trunk opened up like a wing armchair, bore such a crown of mistletoe that its own leaves were eclipsed. Ted looked

Bramble Streamers
ready to take root
along the Rollalong
Drive

askance at that mistletoe, saying that one day it would catch the wind like a sail and the whole tree would blow down. He was right.

It soon became clear that the wind from the west is something to reckon with in winter. The hedges that used to divide the big wheat field were all gone, so my raggedy hedgerow is the first obstacle the wind finds on its way across the low land. On rough days the roar in the treetops is loud enough to be alarming, but so far I have never been there when a dead elm, a living wild plum or an ash branch has come crashing down. If disease spreads and the ash trees in the higher wood die, there will be a lot of crashing.

To fill gaps in the windbreak I tried putting in a mixture of native hedge plants, briar, hazel, dogwood, field maple. But I had not yet got the measure of some of the other natives. Within a short time, all that was left of the young plants was a bristle of bitten stalks. From that experience and a few other early plantings I came to realize that the wood is like the night scene in *Snow White*, with all the animal eyes watching. Nothing I plant is unobserved by the rabbits, deer or mice, and very little is not to their taste. They even chew holly and laurel. Fortifying new plants against my fellow wood-dwellers soon became, and remains, one of the most time-consuming of activities.

Near the entrance to the land is the straightest, youngest-looking of the old apple trees, which I think of as First Tree. It is really two trees in one, the desired original with its huge apples borne on craggy wood up at chimney height, and the more energetic rootstock that forms the trunk and lower branches. The rootstock bears generous amounts of fruit, easy to pick but with no flavour, while the delicious apples are way out of reach. I suppose a fireman could rescue them in an emergency, but I and my ladder get caught up in the clotted branches well below them.

They are fat, round apples, with pronounced folds at the blossom end. From below, they give the impression of a lot of pursed lips looking down in disapproval at my efforts to reach them. So every year they fall, split and spoil on the grass. If I happen to be there I pick up the fresher ones, in competition with wasps, ants, sometimes red admiral butterflies, deer. Those apples cook to an airy, delicious froth.

Mr Scriven had said that he thought that he and his father would have planted all the apples for cider, so my first attempt to have them identified was to visit Julian Temperley of Burrow Hill, cider-maker, and the only holder in this country of a licence to distil apple brandy. Bluff, approachable and, it seemed, rarely free of BBC interviewers, he looked the few apples over till he came to a big double-lobed one from First Tree. He laughed at its buttocks and pushed them all aside, saying he could not recognize any and that I had better send them to Liz Copas, the expert on Somerset cider apples.

Liz Copas used to work at the respected, now mourned, research station at Long Ashton. She wrote *A Somerset Pomona*, a beautiful book over which I have spent long, indecisive moments, pondering if the alignment of pips in a given photograph or the degree of russeting in another could, by any stretch, be said to look like those of the particular specimen I had to hand. I packed up a few leafy twigs with apples attached and sent them to her. Back came a kind letter, saying that it was hard to be sure but that it looked as though Sugg's Orchard was a typical farm orchard with a mixture of cider, cooking and eating apples. She thought the winged armchair tree might be the Rev. Wilks, that the First Tree might be Grenadier, but that some could be nameless seedlings.

Since then other experts have looked, sniffed, tasted, sliced and thought, but not agreed. The name of the Rev. Wilks has reappeared, although not attached to the same tree, various other names have been floated, Warner's King, Lord Suffield, but the overall impression is that identifying apples is far from easy or certain. There are hundreds of varieties, some with names that change from region to region. To begin with, at any rate, it seemed more important to try to restore the frail old trees, or take material to graft from them, than to worry about their names.

When another old apple tree fell over and died after my removal of the elder grown in with it, I had to think again. Perhaps by this stage in the lives of the apple trees, the elder and brambles were more like companion plants than competitors. It seemed better to let the remaining ones be, get on with learning how to graft, and plant afresh where there was new space.

∾

Andrew and his machinery had opened up the first patch of land above the top of the track. I had pictured this as giving a clear rectangle, but for reasons I never asked, a thicket remained in the top left-hand corner, making a lopsided figure not graced with a geometrical name. This made less space for new trees, but it did keep some windbreak and cover for the birds.

In the first season grass grew over this cleared ground. It arrived of its own accord and looked just as it should in an orchard, green, medium-rough, healthy. I was delighted, thinking it would stay like that, but within a blink, nettles, followed by burdock, thistles and a coarse, tussocky grass, came crowding in. I watched with envy the grass being trimmed in Ted's orchard by the cattle. But I live more than a hundred miles away, it was no good thinking about keeping animals as mowers. Or rather, to think of it was a pleasure . . . a couple of rescued donkeys, a pretty little Dexter cow, some rare-breed sheep . . . but only as a daydream. I needed to concentrate on which apple trees to plant.

My cousin had suggested I join the Farmers' Wildlife Advisory Group because of its interest in the conservation of orchards and the grant money in its gift. But, he said, the grants come with strings attached: 'They'll make you do all sorts of things you don't want and it'll end up costing you more.' Still, I did join the advisory group, who recommended the planting of standard trees, because they are traditional for an old orchard.

The closer one gets, the more complicated any subject reveals itself to be. With choosing fruit trees, this process starts with the question of rootstocks. Most fruit trees are grafted on to a rootstock to increase the success and predictability of their performance, the eventual size and vigour of the tree being influenced by the particular rootstock.

That is to say, the grafter cuts off a slim twig, or scion, of the desired tree and binds it on to the cut upright shoot of the appropriate rootstock, so that where the two cuts meet the plants will merge. You will then have the particular variety of tree you want, growing on a rootstock chosen to produce a dwarf, or a middling-sized, or a big tree. It is not that you cannot grow trees from apple pips, just that you have less idea what will emerge – a winner perhaps, like Bramley's Seedling, or a sickly, spindly thing much given to mildew, or a tough, spiny little specimen looking as though it belongs in a hedgerow.

For the traditional standard (big) trees a strong rootstock is needed, but my cousin warned against planting only standards, saying that they grow too tall and take too long to mature. 'You don't want to wait for years, you want to be picking fruit while you're still young enough,' he declared. Is that so, I wondered; leaving aside the unwelcome thought of becoming too old to pick fruit, his words brought into focus the fact that, all being well, I was going to have to think about what to do with the apples. I had not intended to be a fruit producer, but the land I had chanced to buy was an old orchard. With the countryside already bereft of so many of its orchards, I did not want to preside over the final demise of another. Unusual varieties of apple, organically grown, were sure to be saleable in London, I imagined. That became the business plan.

I decided to plant fruit trees of mixed sizes. I ordered my first new apple trees after hours of reading descriptions of the old varieties in the supplier's catalogue. With names like Court Pendu Plat, Dog's Snout, Peasgood's Nonsuch, Cornish Gilliflower, it was hard to resist ordering twice as many as there was room for. However, a long telephone conversation with the nurseryman, during which I could sense both patience and impatience at the other end of the line, produced a list: Annie Elizabeth, Lord Derby, Orleans Reinette and London Pippin, plus a medlar, Nottingham. All, I was assured, perfect for damp West Country land. Thinking millennially, I had hoped to plant them in 2000 but the ground was too wet, so they had to wait till February 2001.

I collected the trees from the nursery on a raw, wintry day, crossing over a border of disinfected straw at the gateway. The foot-and-mouth epidemic had not been going long but it was already tearing at the heart of the farming community around there. The nurseryman seemed distracted, dismayed, even though he was not a farmer. Annie Elizabeth, I was told, was unavailable so I was getting Keswick Codlin instead. After all the earlier deliberations, the careful choice of varieties, I was surprised to hear, 'They're much the same, anyway.' The nurseryman's dog, friendlier and more relaxed than its owner, kept me company during the chill wait for the trees to be fetched.

They were only small, *maidens* in the quaint terminology, and fitted easily on the back seat of the car. It was with the feeling of quitting an area gripped by plague that I left for the thirty-mile drive back to Aller, to which, mercifully, foot-and-mouth disease never came.

∾

In honour of Sir Thomas Browne and his *The Garden of Cyrus*, I was determined to plant the new trees in the form of the quincunx. With only four apple trees this would have been tricky, but the existing First Tree was there to make up the figure. It was years since I had been bewildered and delighted by Browne's essay, so I looked it up. A second reading of *The Garden of Cyrus or, The Quincuncial Lozenge, or Network Plantations of the Ancients, Artificially, Naturally, Mystically Considered by Thomas Browne D. of Physick printed in the year 1658* proved just as stretching as the first.

In terms of a planting guide it is simple. The trees are placed at five points as they appear on a playing card, the five of clubs, for example. This is repeated to make a pattern of offset rows. Apart from planting in a square pattern, it is the most likely arrangement for an orchard. The only genius required was to spin out that simplicity into seventy-five pages of allusion, argument, speculation and resounding language.

Casting back into antiquity for a model gardener, Browne has to dismiss Adam as coming too late to have laid out the Garden of Eden, remarking, 'Gardens were before Gardiners.' Cyrus, the Persian king, is the earliest model he can find: 'All

stories do look upon Cyrus, as the splendid and regular planter.'
To be precise, as Browne always seeks to be, the younger of two
Cyruses: 'Not only a Lord of Gardens, but a manuall planter
thereof: disposing his trees like his armies in regular ordination . . . the rows and orders so handsomely disposed; or five
trees so set together, that a regular angularity, and through
prospect, was left on every side.'

After this Browne rather loses sight of Cyrus in pursuit of the
exact sort of X that can be drawn between the five points of the
figure. He goes on to mention any number of things he says he
is not going to mention, to find quincunxes hither and yon in
nature, 'how nature Geometrizeth, and observeth order in all
things' (although perhaps he had no cat, as he misses out the
quincuncial alignment of a cat's whiskers), then to comment on
instances of five as a mystical number. Until, almost at last, he
writes his wonderful lines, 'But the Quincunx of Heaven runs
low, and 'tis time to close the five ports of knowledge.' I put
down the book with the feeling of having been led home after
an erratic, fantastical adventure. Not that it had made much
difference to the way I would lay out my trees, or that I had
much hope of disposing them like armies in regular ordination,
but it was warming to know that anyone, ever, had found the
topic so rich.

Digging planting holes in my land is hard. There is little top-
soil, so a spade reaches dull, mustard-coloured clay in no time.
Just under the surface, the earth is a network of roots, yellow
ropes of nettle, dark thongs of wild plum and thorn, that show
bright orange-red when cut. Pinkish worms, much smaller than
the luxuriant ones that live in garden soil, labour their lives
away in this dense, close world. I soon developed the habit of
digging with a fork first, because it is easier but also less likely
to slice through worms, my allies in this tiring soil.

How hard people have worked and still work, the world over, breaking in virgin soil, making fields from forest, with only their own labour. No wonder they turned to enslaving animals, or each other, or later to machinery. These thoughts soon struck me as I began, although mine was not virgin soil, just neglected. Ted lent me a mattock, the classic tool for breaking soil by hand, but I failed to get into the swing of it. Anyway, I only needed holes, not expanses of open ground, and it was a slicer of worms.

The planting holes filled with water as I was digging them. My cousin had warned against autumn planting for that very reason: 'You might as well stand bare roots in a bucket of water and watch them rot,' but now I had the trees to plant and it would soon be March, so they had to go in. I prowled the wheat field, picking up stones to drop into the bottom of the 'buckets', and dug drainage channels to draw off the water. It seemed to work, so in went the trees and their stakes, with a bag of compost for their roots, a spiral rabbit guard round their trunks, a piece of old carpet to deter the weeds and a surround of chicken wire to keep out the deer. Each tree took much longer than expected; it was good I had bought so few.

However, those trees were not the only ones to go in that year. Ashmead's Kernel and a quince, Meech's Prolific, joined them, in what was meant to be an extension of the quincuncial pattern but had to step out of line round the remaining scrub.

Collecting those trees from Robin Small, of Charlton Orchards, was a cheerful experience. In the cool of his packing shed, muffled up in a scarf and a thick white Guernsey sweater, Robin seemed to have no more pressing thing to do than tell me how he became a fruit-grower. Nothing in his background, Robin said, had pointed him in the direction of apples. He was in the Merchant Navy but there was a girl he wanted to marry and be at home with. He thought and thought about what line to pursue until one day, up on deck, 'I think a little apple molecule must have floated by, because I suddenly thought, that's it, I'll be an apple-grower.' So he took a correspondence course, came home, and he and June started to look for land.

The land they found was east of Taunton. As a young couple they settled in, joining a small rural community, one that was soon to be shaken by the arrival of new housing and many more outsiders. At the time of my visit, June had just written an illustrated history of the village. Her research for it, so Robin related, seemed to have been the first occasion on which anyone had asked the original families what they felt about the abrupt expansion of their village.

As he spoke, Robin trimmed the quince he was selling me, snipping twigs with a beautiful old pair of secateurs. They were small enough to nestle in his palm, all of metal with the dull shine that comes of being much handled. He said that he sharpened them twice a day. I was impressed. Never in my life had I thought of sharpening secateurs.

∾

With the foot-and-mouth epidemic still spreading, travel in the countryside was discouraged. My young maidens, protected by their plastic rabbit guards and wire enclosures, were left to themselves for a while. When I next visited some months later it was to discover that something had got in under the wire of the Keswick Codlin and taken on the challenge of the spiral plastic guard. Rough tooth marks and tears followed each other in a spiral up the bark of the young Keswick Codlin.

I looked at the damage, wondering if the tree would live, if spiral barking amounts to ring barking. But that little tree has turned out to be a survivor. The next setback it suffered was canker, a fungal disease causing lesions and swellings of the bark, sometimes bad enough for the branch beyond the canker to die off. Because it developed almost straight away I was inclined to blame the supplier, but my cousin said that all old West Country orchards have canker, that it comes with the wind and rain, and anyway, not to fret. Cut out the worst and let the tree carry on, was his advice, which is not what the books say. They take a more alarmist view.

Keswick Codlin's leading shoot was cankered, quite low down. To cut it out would mean deforming for ever the way the tree would grow. With a heavy heart and no great conviction that it would not make things worse, I sawed it off. It looked, and continues to look, a disgrace. Anyone who wanted their orchard to be like an army in regular ordination would have thrown it out.

～

The more I got going in the wood the more tools I needed, but once the Rollalong was in place they could be kept in its separate compartment. This tall, narrow space, designed to house a chemical toilet, was empty except for a hook and an old coin glued, inexplicably, to the wall. With stuff piled in, it soon took on the air of slippage that any bare shed invites. The new stainless-steel spade and fork, the rake and the hoe might manage to stay upright in a corner, but the plastic spiral tree guards lolled and splayed over the slouching bags of compost on the floor. Everything else had either to balance on top or, more often, slide down out of sight between or behind them. A roll of black weed-suppressing fabric stood in another corner, its end unfurling like a gloomy banner.

Some sort of moth must soon have found that that roll of black fabric was just right for its grubs. It was only later that I saw what impressive progress they had made through the outside layers, before retiring to the inner darkness to pupate. Small brown moths, like outsize clothes moths, fluttered free as I unrolled their erratic lacework. As so often in my encounters with the wood's wildlife, I wondered how they manage their affairs. How did they know that within that locked cubicle, accessible perhaps through the air vent, lay the sort of fabric to suit their needs?

The obvious remedy to the squalor of the tool store would have been to put up shelves and racks, but the two inner walls looked flimsy, so might not have supported much weight. Instead, some form of free-standing furniture seemed a better idea. I had no clear mental picture of this until, back in London and walking along Holloway Road, what should I happen to see? There, by a street tree, was a small gathering of things no longer wanted in a stationer's shop. Most were easy to ignore, but my eye was drawn to the elegance of a dark-blue metal display stand, discreetly boasting, 'Oxford, the World's Most Trusted Dictionaries'.

I stopped to consider this object. It was quite tall, with four deep shelves, but maybe not too tall to fit into the Rollalong. It appeared to be sound, it even had castors. It cannot have been thrown out for long, no banana skins or paper cups had yet been shelved. It also had, for all its Oxford-blue sobriety, a flourish at the top where the dome of the Bodleian Library put in an appearance, cut out in sheet metal, with loose brushstrokes of white to indicate the dome's ribs and embellishments. It was altogether promising.

I checked with the shopkeeper that it was indeed a throw-out. 'Please, take, take,' he said. So I took, pushing my prize over the paving slabs and kerbs, wondering whether it would survive the half-mile it had to travel. But those castors had been made to carry the weight of four shelves of dictionaries. It may have been the last triumph of their trundling days that they took so well to the hazards of the London streets.

In height, the display case fitted into the tool store as though made to measure, and its narrowness turned out to be an advantage when my next acquisition, a gangly, awkward-shaped strimmer, needed to slip in beside it. Strimmer or brush-cutter, the two names overlap in denoting the same sort of machine, the one worn slung over one shoulder, held with a big, bowed handlebar and swung from side to side.

I bought the strimmer at the Bridgwater branch of Mole Valley, a farmers' co-operative, where you can buy anything from horse medicaments to baby clothes, galvanized cattle troughs to marigolds; even mole traps, despite the cheery mole on the logo. Mostly what I buy is simple, thick woolly socks, wire, tree guards or wooden stakes, but on the strimmer occasion I was in need of guidance and sought out a salesman.

Our conversation about strimmers had reached a narrowing point when the salesman revealed that the machine we appeared to be choosing came flat-packed, that it required self-assembly. My expression must have conveyed that an imminent sale was about to turn to dust, but the man rose to the moment. He was not meant to assemble things for customers, he explained, but he was new to the job and it would be good for him to put this item together so he could advise about it in the future.

We made a conspiratorial huddle in the corner with the plumbing sundries. With a few sidelong glances to see that he was not being watched, he set to. The work did not look like complete child's play. It took a while, and involved some of the bemused comparison between instruction sheet and actual object integral to self-assembly. But it took nothing like as long as it would have done in my hands, and the result looked convincing. I hope the salesman knew how grateful I was, how without his help I might have walked out crestfallen, strimmerless.

For a while afterwards I would see that salesman in the store, but then we either stopped recognizing each other, or he left. Or perhaps he hid as soon as he saw me coming, the glint of a new quest, a chainsaw, in my eye. I have wasted plenty of time, my own and other people's, stringing out chainsaw conversations, but never yet to the point of buying one.

'What do you want it for?' is the usual first question. The answer is, for clearing small trees or branches and cutting up firewood. But for the echo of a story told to me years ago, I could give the more succinct reply, 'for limbing'. It was a true story, once the talk of the area around my cousin's farm. 'For limbing' was the reason a wronged husband gave for buying a chainsaw. He was being literal. A tree survives limbing, but the man's rival did not.

The surprising thing about chainsaws is not, obviously, that they can be lethal but that they are so heavy. Young men flip them about like wands, but a chainsaw powerful enough to be of much use is a chunky beast. That is the main reason I walk out of stores without one, but fear comes into it too, and impatience with all the safety suit, the gloves, the headgear, the footwear. But it would be wrong to say that by the time one had done all that dressing up, a handsaw would have been quicker. I watch with envy the speed of a chainsaw flying through green wood.

∾

After a few seasons I was asked to give a talk about the wood to a gardening club in London. The focus was not to be on apples, or tree-planting, but on flowers. What flowers? I soon wondered. With no swathes of anything except weeds to lyricize about, little that could be termed gardening even attempted and late summer already passing, I was going to have to make a few reed heads, thistle tops, rosehips and wisps of old man's beard go a long way.

The first decision was to present anything that was in flower or going attractively to seed, without getting categorical about weeds, wild flowers or woodland gardening. This allowed me, for the purposes of the talk, to sidestep the question of what plants are, or are not, suitable to grow. In other words, how much to treat the wood like a garden.

The next decision was technical. At that time photographic slides were still current but already old-fashioned. For an alluring moment I pictured myself with a digital camera, breezy in the face of PowerPoint. But then the thought of how little time there was for this transformation, of the ill temper and panic it would entail, meant that the old camera won out.

You might expect a four-acre space that had been left to itself for fifty years to be teeming with diverse plant life, but conservation-minded visitors have not been impressed. However, these were there already, or came of their own accord once more light had been let in: ground ivy, nettles, stinking iris, buttercup, thistles (various), grasses (various), false oxlip, bugle, mint, violets, water figwort, loosestrife, willow herb, sedge, rush, dog rose, meadowsweet, hemp agrimony, honeysuckle, orchid, dandelion, burnet, burdock, old man's beard, briony, hart's tongue fern, lords and ladies, spurge laurel, celandine, hawk-bit, ivy, dogwood, woody nightshade, forget-me-not, comfrey, groundsel, garlic, ragwort, shepherd's purse, vetch, daisy, enchanter's nightshade, cleavers, avens, cow parsley, speedwell, fleabane, bramble, lady's smock, lemon balm, periwinkle, pignut. Mullein and foxgloves turned up once but not again, and there are many more plants I cannot identify, along with mosses, lichens, fungi.

As I stepped round with a camera on a late-September day, very few of these were even visible, let alone photogenic. But the bright-orange seeds of the stinking iris looked good, held proud as the sections of the seed-head began to arc open among the dark-green pointed leaves. Stinking iris is an unfair name. There is no smell unless the plant is crushed, its flower is pretty in a subtle way. But still, wild-flower books tend to be dismissive of it. Here is the nineteenth-century clergyman and headmaster, the Rev. C. A. Johns, whose *Flowers of the Field* (1907 edition), came to me along with my aunt's fluted teapot and silvery vacuum flask. On the subject of *Iris foetidissima* he writes: 'The flowers are of a dull leaden hue, and the leaves so acrid as to leave a burning taste in the mouth, or even to loosen the teeth. The whole plant when bruised emits a disagreeable odour.' He does admit that the seeds, 'arranged in some quaint jar or vase (without water), remain a pleasing and decorative object throughout the winter'.

Now where did he get that bit about loosening the teeth from? Did he, in the name of science, try eating the leaves himself as he sat at his headmasterly desk, admiring those seed-heads in their quaint jar? The animals in the wood leave that iris alone, although something smaller, toothless already perhaps, likes their leaves, working through them, turning them brown.

Lords-and-ladies, cuckoo-pint or wake-robin, the little arum that comes up early in the year all over the wood, is another plant the animals shun. But later in the season it is often hidden by grass, making the elegant, filmy sheath round the fruiting parts vulnerable to being slashed down, so that only a few get as far as flaunting their bright-red berries in the autumn. I had to clamber in among their protection of twiggy debris to photograph them.

Another plant that was fairly easy to reach with the camera was mistletoe. Mistletoe is a plant hard to categorize: it could be a weed, a wild flower, a parasite, a crop, a blessing. Whether it is a weed or not, in damp West Country orchards it grows like one. I always liked mistletoe, but, having become a keeper of old apple trees, am more critical of it than before, when it was just a part of Christmas. Or, as the Rev. C. A. Johns puts it, at the season when 'it is the symbol of a strange spirit of superstitious frivolity too well known to need description'. More than a century after he wrote that, a description might have been helpful. Is it just kissing he means, or were there other mistletoe frivolities, now forgotten?

My current misgivings about mistletoe are all to do with the way the wind catches it. Left to itself, mistletoe grows into such vibrant big bundles that the winter winds, instead of hurrying through bare branches, buffet and toss them about until the lot can come down, mistletoe, branch, even the whole tree. If the tree dies, so does the mistletoe, leaving a sad mess of stubby ends, or 'bone-like joints', as the Reverend saw them. So to have someone to harvest the mistletoe is a useful thing.

One November afternoon, I stayed on in the Rollalong. With candles blazing, tea, things to note down, I had not noticed how dark it was getting. When I got up to leave I realized that it was very dark. On winter evenings there is usually a glimmer of light, enough to make out the rabbit holes along the path before getting out in the open, but this particular evening was darker. Not having a torch, I lit a candle lantern and set off. The lantern shed very little light but it was a comfort.

Apple Tree with too much Mistletoe

All went well until I was surprised to see, from the top of the track, some sort of vehicle parked at the bottom. A pale glow was spilling from inside, the engine was running but the road lights were switched off. Getting nearer I could see that it was a flatbed truck piled high with mistletoe. Thieves! Mistletoe Rustlers! I had heard enough local stories to be instantly afraid someone was up to No Good.

I cannot now recapture why it was so disconcerting to see, as I inched past the right-hand side of the cab, a large image of a face blurrily reflected on the inside of the steamed-up windscreen, upside down, if I am now recalling it correctly. The image was of a man shaving, a domestic enough scene, but it quite undid any nerve I might have had for challenging his right to be there. And, villain or no, it seemed rude to rap on the door if he was shaving. So past I tiptoed with my lantern, slid into the car and escaped. Before going home I called in at Ted's house in Aller to report what I had seen.

'Oh that's all right, that's only the mistletoe man,' exclaimed Doreen. She said that he and his son came all the way from Cambridge every year to pick mistletoe from various old orchards, and that Ted let them stay in the yard. She smiled when she heard I had been so scared.

The next year I met the mistletoe man in person, in the light, and we laughed not only about how alarmed I had been, but also about how he and his son were startled by the will-o'-the-wisp lantern appearing out of the darkness, wavering by with never a word. For the next few years we would enjoy recalling that moment, and agreeing on how much we liked Ted, 'a lovely boy, a proper old countryman', as the mistletoe man put it.

But then he stopped coming. Doreen says that he got too old and his son did not want to continue, there being little money in mistletoe, at least for the gatherer. So the mistletoe in the old trees in Ted's orchard gets thicker, and, year by year, down come more trees. Even at the time of meeting the mistletoe man, I was aware of feeling lucky, that this was an encounter with, as it were, a journeyman from the rural past.

ॐ

The talk about flowers in the wood went cheerfully enough. Among the gardeners of an inner-London borough were a good number who either already had, or would like to have, their hands on a bigger patch of wilder land than was available to them in London, so they were sympathetic. If there was impatience in the suggestion from one brusque old woman that the best way to deal with the brambles would be to set light to them, another voice immediately spoke up in defence of the bramble-dwellers.

These people, nearly all women, were residents of what was then reputed to be the least green borough in London. Perhaps that was why no one at that gathering posed the sort of challenging question about the wood that I had recently been asked by a friend. This friend and I had been shimmying through shoulder-high weeds on our way to the hazel wood, if not in comfort, in what had appeared to be perfect harmony. But then she rebelled, came to a sudden halt and, gesticulating around her, exclaimed, 'What is all this *for?*'

Taken aback, I could think of nothing to say, other than to apologize about the lack of a mown path. What *was* it for? All I knew, deep within those layers of being that are no good at yielding answers, was . . . that I had taken up this quixotic pursuit because I wanted to. The wood, a beautiful, unmanageable place, had already become so much a part of me that it seemed to need no explanation. Later on, when things were somewhat more in hand, I was pleased to hear this same friend say, 'I couldn't see it before, but I get it now.'

Even today, if asked to explain the wood, I still grope about for words. Lately I have been trying out *solace*. Solace, not because I reckon my circumstances to have been hard. In the scale of the world's hardships, mine has been a feather-bed. Nonetheless, loss is loss, grief is grief, and everyday life is rich in reverses. Some find consolation in religion or meditation, but I prefer to be out of doors, quietly busy.

I am not sure why we humans should take comfort from the natural world, harsh and implacable as it is, but there is something very buoyant about the company of trees, plants, animals, birds, insects, all intent upon their own lives. As far as we know they just get on with it, having offspring, trying not to starve, not to be eaten, without asking *why*. Perhaps some of this buoyancy transmits itself, helps keep us afloat too. My oldest friend from schooldays touched my heart recently when she exclaimed that she loves being in the wood, how it makes her happy just to be there. That is how I feel, too.

Looking down into Ted's orchard

Chapter 6

Weeds, Flowers and the Opening-Up of Long Hill Orchard

But this little patch which lies facing east . . .
Was full – of nettles! All over
My small piece of land they grew, their barbs
Tipped with a smear of tingling poison.
What should I do? So thick were the ranks
That grew from the tangle of roots below,
They were like the green hurdles a stableman skilfully
Weaves of pliant osiers when the horses' hooves
Rot in the standing puddles and go soft as fungus.
So I put it off no longer. I set to work with my mattock
And dug the sluggish ground from their embraces.
I tore those nettles though they grew and grew again.
I destroyed the tunnels of the moles that haunt dark places,
And back to the realms of light I summoned the worms.

THE HORTULUS OF WALAHFRID STRABO,
C.840, TRANSLATED FROM LATIN BY RAEF PAYNE

THERE YOU ARE, WELL AWARE OF which century it is, when suddenly someone from another time or place is there too, keeping you company; to me that is one of the great joys of reading. I first became a nettle-owner more than eleven centuries after Walahfrid Strabo had confronted his, but as my nettles grew and grew again, he stood, as it were, at my shoulder.

Walahfrid, poet, monk, one-time tutor to Charlemagne's great-nephew, returned from his employment out in the great world to the Benedictine abbey of his childhood, Reichenau, to become its abbot. In his poem about nettles and gourds, irises and wormwood, roses and betony, he speaks as a practical grower and herbalist. Which is unusual, personal records of early gardeners being rare.

Walahfrid died in 849, the same year that Alfred the Great was born. I would like to spin a web to link the two, to have Alfred reading Walahfrid's poem, or placing it in the library of his new abbey at Athelney. I could project an even more improbable web to include Sugg's Orchard. But I will keep to the nettles. Whether in the first or third millennium, there is nothing like a nettle to bring you down to earth.

Nettles like green hurdles of pliant osier are a surprise, though. However thick they grow, mine never feel like a hurdle. But where my experience coincides with Walahfrid's is in the nettle's capacity to withstand efforts to eradicate it. At first I hoped that a really good try at clearing a patch of ground, till there seemed to be not a thread of yellow root left, would work. When it did not, I watched the area around Ted's sheds where he would use weed-killer. The tops of the nettles duly died off and looked forlorn. But the roots must have been alive, because back came new shoots later on.

At this point in my acquaintance with my nettles, several seasons after I had taken over the land, it seemed better to think of forming an entente cordiale with them. They provide, after all, a food source for the caterpillars of peacock and small tortoiseshell butterflies, several moths and indeed us, if you like eating leaves with a furry texture. Then there are the nettle teas, the yarn, the rope and the noxious-smelling plant food all made from them. As I surveyed my expanses of nettle, the thought did occur that perhaps these weeds were a crop.

At that time the shops of Culpeper the Herbalist had not yet disappeared, so I rang to ask if they were interested in buying nettles. The answer was, well yes, but only when dried and graded. Feeling that the harvesting and drying of nettles might not be fun, I tried to keep the topic alive by asking, what did a buyer look for in a first-class dried nettle? There was no clear reply to this, only a feeling of lethargy descending upon the conversation.

Commercial or not, the nettle growth up at the wood is so strong that I have sought to understand why they do so well there, at least in the areas open to the light. Nettles, it is widely said, like the ground around human habitations, because where humans live, animals often live. Over time, with one sort of waste and another, a good, rich, nitrogenous soil builds up. There is no reason to suppose that humans have lived on that land, but pigs have. Andrew recalls working after school for old Mr Scriven, hefting buckets of water up to the pigs.

What with pig manure, the damp ground and now the light, the nettles have just what they want. But not everything goes their way. Mowing discourages them and, disliking weight on their roots, they started to dwindle along the most frequently

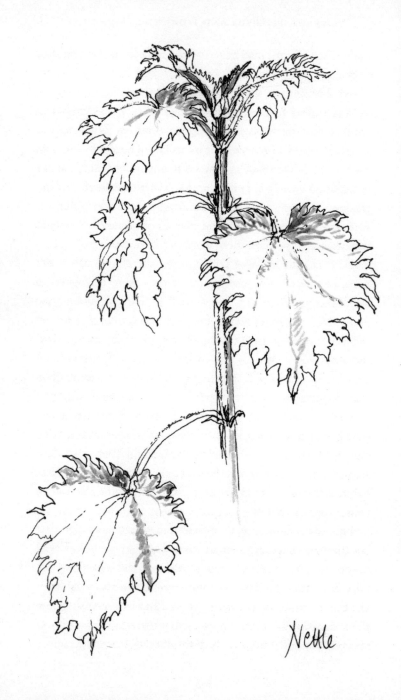

Nettle

used paths. I know that this is temporary, that they would be back in a flash if they had the chance, but for now I have learnt to live with them.

There are, however, plants I would much rather live with, bluebells, for instance. What is it about bluebells that makes people ask, with longing, 'Is it a bluebell wood?' No one asks if it is a snowdrop wood, or a wood of any other flower. Maybe it has to do with that particular shade of blue, the blue of the Madonna's robe, or the untethered way the colour seems to swirl just above the woodland floor, more mauve than blue when seen massed together. Whatever it is we do seem to find magic in the idea of a bluebell wood, so I was happy, early on, to see a few bluebell leaves appearing near the entrance at the top of the track.

By the next time I was there, the leaves had been sawn off in a neat line, so neat that it looked as though someone had taken shears to them. Assuming the shears to have been teeth, I wondered whose teeth, because bluebells are bad for rabbits and deer. Certainly the shearing was bad for the bluebells, although they still linger in that place, surviving the rough treatment they get from scuffling feet as well as teeth. Sometimes they have been allowed to flower, their flowers revealing that they are not of the desired native kind, bluest-blue with an arching habit, but one of the stubbier hybrids often dismissed with conservationist hauteur as *Spanish*.

I bought bulbs that were supposed to be of native bluebells but they too came up pale and straight, got in the way of burrowers, were damaged and failed to spread. Further along the ridge English bluebells thrive in the scruffy woods of a Ministry of Defence firing range, where conditions look no better for them than in my wood, unless perhaps the rabbits get shot. Might a few bulbs from there transplant all right? Years ago, to have stepped into that wood, lifted half a dozen bulbs and replanted them two miles away would not have sounded outrageous. Now even to think of it is almost criminal. So no, it is not a bluebell wood. Nor a snowdrop wood, although that failing I have, since my first winter there, been trying harder to remedy.

It needs about a century's worth of undisturbed growth to get a proper, dense acreage of snowdrops, so thick underfoot that you can hardly help treading on them. Unless, that is, you really go at it with the planting, or devote plenty of time afterwards to splitting up the clumps and replanting. I read that in a Gloucestershire garden *a hundred thousand snowdrops were planted in one autumn alone*. Note the passive voice. How I salute those nameless autumnal planters of the hundred thousand. A hundred is nearer the mark for me.

A friend of my aunt's, the widow of a country doctor and an admirer of gypsies, told me that if you see masses of snowdrops growing on a verge or spreading into roadside woodland, that means gypsies used to camp there. They planted and picked the snowdrops as a crop. If only they had done so on my patch.

The first snowdrops I planted in the wood were doubles from under the chestnut tree in my farming cousin's garden. They dwindled near the Rollalong, but have come up every year under the apple, First Tree. Living among tree roots seems to suit them. Every February I add more bulbs, *in the green*, some given, some bought, some common, some choice. I put them in all over the place in the hope that they will one day meet up in a continuous swathe.

It would be reasonable to expect the common ones to be doing better, but my most successful snowdrop so far has a distinguished background, coming from the collection of the great gardener E. A. Bowles of Myddelton House, Enfield. Mr Bowles loved snowdrops. He planted many varieties in his rock garden, which then enjoyed decades of benign neglect after his death in 1954. For a brief, happy interlude early in this century you could visit the resultant wealth of snowdrops, spread like a snowy coverlet over the soft mounds of the buried rock garden, then buy polythene bags of a few unlabelled bulbs, with the cheery comment that it was pot luck, you could be getting a great rarity for all anyone knew.

I was lucky enough to have come away with some of those bags. A delicate, yellow-marked variety failed, but a tall one, a *plicatus* I later learnt, took to the ivy-covered bank at the top of the hazel wood. It is a place where sunshine can reach in winter, before the hazel leaves open into great shady saucers. There Mr Bowles's snowdrop flourishes. It flowers quite early, on tall stems, then its leaves go on to form a grey-green cascade down the bank.

One winter I happened to be staying in an old house in Argyll. There was much to admire there, but to me it was the spread and vigour of the snowdrops and the size of the rabbits that were most striking. The snowdrops were everywhere, in any little crevice between tree roots, clambering the stony banks that bordered the farmland, flattened under the tyres of cars parked beside the drive. They were of the common, single sort, but uncommonly healthy. The current owners of the house did not know who had planted them, or when. To them the snowdrops were a minor, self-sustaining detail of a big project. To me they seemed a marvellous gift.

Nor did the owners find their rabbits remarkable. But those rabbits looked huge, at least in comparison with my Somerset ones. I wondered about them; were they just extra-furry because of the Scottish cold but the same small size inside, or were they really bigger? Why did they look so much more robust? Given that the Somerset ones suffer from myxomatosis every so often, were these bonny Scots ones immune? Again, no one seemed to know. Those rabbits did not appear to be eating snowdrops, although I am not sure that mine do either. I find shredded snowdrop leaves, bitten flowers and the bulbs tossed out of the ground, but there are snails, squirrels, mice and doubtless other creatures. What was obvious, there in Argyll, was that fine snowdrops and fine rabbits could coexist.

I had no wish to import the rabbits, but was delighted to be given some of the snowdrops. They are growing, but even were I to live to a hundred and fifty, I doubt if I would see them in such triumphant abundance as in that Scottish garden. Most snowdrops originated up in the mountains of Greece, Turkey, the Caucasus. Maybe Argyll feels more like home to them than does a ridge above the Somerset Levels.

❧

In about 2005, Ted made me an offer. He and his son, Philip, would reinstate the lost, overgrown boundary between our two properties if I paid for the fence posts and barbed wire. He had some health worries and wanted to make sure his orchard was in good order while he was still able. This, as things were to turn out, was wise of him. As though the idea of a new fence needed promotion, he added with a sly smile, 'I can get green wire, you'll probably like that better.'

I suspected that Ted took a satirical view of my refusal to use weed-killer. Could this green wire be some environmentally friendly version of barbed wire, I wondered, or was the green an aesthetic consideration? I thanked him, saying green would be nice, and awaited the outcome. The wire, when it came, looked

Snowdrops & Catkins

like any other barbed wire, except it had the pale, icy-green sheen of homemade peppermint creams.

For much of its length, the old fence was invisible underneath mounds of bramble. These brambles continued up in unchallenged possession over the Long Hill Orchard part of my land. This was the area I had never penetrated, that my brother called the New Territories. Ted and Philip's work was about to open up a new chapter.

As well as the derelict fence and brambles, there were the remains of older ways of marking the boundary, a bank with a mixture of ash, hawthorn and elm trees outgrown from a hedge, their lower trunks deformed and twisted from having been cut back so often. It was late summer when Philip began to clear for the fencing work, his digger chewing into the undergrowth along this margin, leaving the standing trees and opening a walk as far as the big ash that Ted recognized as marking the extent of my property.

I saw none of this activity; it was October before I could come and look at what had been happening. Arriving from London about an hour before dark, it was in soft evening light that I first stepped along this broad, new path. I was jubilant. There was the new fence, but much better, the new views that had opened up. I could look over farmland towards Langport to the south-east, swing my eyes past the Curry Rivel escarpment and the hills beyond, then south-westwards across the plain of the River Parrett. It was too dusky to see Pitt's monument to William Pynsent, but the blur of Aller Church was there, if you knew where to look for it. Indeed most of this view was already half familiar, although I had not been able to see it all at once before. But further round, before the view to the north-west was cut off by a curtain of trees, I picked out from the felty evening greyness a dark conical shape . . . Burrow Mump.

Burrow Mump is a small hill with a ruined church on top, a poor man's Glastonbury, a few miles further along the River Parrett at Burrowbridge. It is there that a seventeenth-century man's bones were found, thought to have been buried after either the Battle of Langport or the Battle of Sedgemoor. The mound is spotlit at night and can be seen like a spectre in the blackness from the London-bound train. I had had no idea it would be visible from the wood, and greeted it as an unexpected friend.

In truth, the view from the top of the ridge, to which my land does not extend, is far better than from where I was standing. From up there, the power lines and pylons crossing Aller Moor are hardly noticeable. I do try to love those pylons, to appreciate them as the triumph of Modernist design some are able to see. At least they are not solid; one can see through and beyond them to the hazy lines of hills in their layered progression that make me think of Italy.

My brother was incredulous when I remarked upon that, but then I felt vindicated on hearing that the Italian prisoners of war who used to work on the farms along the ridge were also reminded of Italy by that view. There is a bronze sculpture standing on a high plinth beside a road crossing the Mendips, of the she-wolf suckling Romulus and Remus. Made by one of the Italian prisoners, it commemorates their presence in Somerset.

Some of those prisoners came to like Somerset, or perhaps it was a girl they liked, or they could see that making a living there was not so hard as it was at home. At any rate, a few of them settled after the war. I happened to meet the son of one when buying supplies in Bridgwater. As he counted out tree stakes from what looked like a heap of giant pencils, he related how his father had gone back to Calabria as soon as he could, had gathered up his wife and a brother or two and returned to Somerset, to work in a factory in Bridgwater.

Soon they had a greenhouse and were growing, to the surprise of their neighbours, a profusion of tomatoes, peppers, aubergines, courgettes, basil. I remarked that people from southern Europe tend to despise tomatoes grown here, too far from the sweetening sun. But he said that, even in England, his father's tomatoes had always been wonderful. I asked if he still grew them. 'Yes, but not like my dad.'

An owl was calling as I paced about the newly opened length of land on my side of the fence, hemmed in by the grey-purple wall of remaining bramble. In the failing light the soil along this strip looked rough, but not altogether wrecked by the passage of the digger. The digger was still parked near the ponies' stable. If I were to ask Philip before he took it away on another job, perhaps he could open up another acre or so for tree-planting.

I had qualms about this trajectory, from only wanting to work by hand, through accepting the need for smallish machinery, to welcoming in a digger. But I had owned the land for more than five years, long enough to know that the New Territories were not going to yield to a pair of secateurs. And, if Philip would be doing that, might it not make sense to ask him to dig the pond out as well?

☙

Later, when Philip and his digger had come and gone and huge bonfires had burnt for days on end, Ted remarked, 'The number of robins that came out of those brambles, you wouldn't believe.' At which I felt sorry for the robins and whatever other living things I had made homeless, and promised that that was it, there would be no more big clearances. Of the area I had bought, about half was now open, although not in any regular fashion, and so it has remained.

The only occasion on which I was there to see Philip and his digger in action was when he scooped out and extended the pond. The pond as Mr Scriven had left it was so obscured by elder and brambles that it had taken a long time to find. Once brought back to light, it resembled a grey drawstring pouch, the top end being where the spring water trickled between ferns down Mr Scriven's narrow stone inlet, the pouch being the plump body of fine-grain sludge, with only a skim of clear water over the top. Putting so much as a stick in it, let alone a booted foot, stirred up a charcoal-coloured fog.

It was, in other words, extremely zuggy. You could deduce rather than see where the outlet was, because of the hand-basin-sized hollow of water I had once hoped was the spring. This hollow lay between the pond and the ditch, along the line of the buried drain.

The pond was only small, just a watering hole for the animals. Like many a new landowner before and after me, I wanted it bigger. Not huge, but with enough space for a miniature island in the middle. And on the island, a summerhouse, a duck-house, a bridge, and who knows what else besides.

The contrast was amazing, between my previous experiments poking about in the zug with a spade, and Philip swinging in with the digger. In minutes he had wrenched up great bucketfuls of clay and vegetation, while I looked on with equal excitement and alarm.

With its cover so abruptly removed, the lie of the land round the pond was easier to see. There was no denying that it was too steep for an island. If I had insisted on having one, the water on the north side would have lain far down between steep sides, a sort of Corinth Canal. So we compromised on a kidney shape with half an island, an isthmus, in the middle. Philip finished the work after I had left, remarking later that it was surprising how quickly the pond filled once he had banged the exposed clay down with the back of the digger scoop.

With what high excitement did I approach it on my next visit. Rawness, rather than serene beauty, is to be expected of a recent excavation, but it was the thought of all that new expanse of spring water that was hastening my steps, round the twist and turn of trees that conceal the pond from the entrance.

The good thing was that the pond was full. Less good was that it was still very small. Absence had allowed it to grow bigger in my imagination, but looking at it afresh, I thought I should have been bolder. Also, the water was far from limpid. Not only was it strewn with an understandable mash of damaged leaves and twigs, but a displeasing, milky film had formed across the surface. If Mr Scriven had been right about that water being exceptionally pure, it hardly looked it. But perhaps the film was only temporary, perhaps it would clear.

I had brought some roots of yellow flags and blue Siberian iris. The idea was to plant the flag irises right into the water and the Siberian ones above the margins of water and bank. But some premonition made me feel uncertain about the constancy of this margin, how high or low the water would remain, so I planted some roots higher than others. However, no such premonition interrupted my fantasy of a summerhouse on the isthmus, where the ground was fairly flat.

This summerhouse notion had been with me for a long time, egged on by a chance postcard from Sweden. The postcard showed the *lusthus* of Ebba Brahe. Perched on a white footbridge, reflected in clear water in all its pink-and-white prettiness, this dreamlike confection was, I believe, Ebba Brahe's writing room. The footbridge appears to span a lake from a bank to an island. The summerhouse dates from 1636, and so has long outlived its original occupant, who died in 1674. That such a fragile-looking structure, poised only just above water, has survived suggests a near-miracle of maintenance.

When they were both young, Ebba Brahe and King Gustavus Adolphus loved each other. Left to their own devices they would have married, but Ebba Brahe was only a lady-in-waiting, and Swedish. The king's mother preferred to play for something more strategic on the chessboard of European royalty. Popular legend presented Ebba and the king as star-crossed lovers, but that did not stop her from marrying someone else, having numerous children and becoming very good at managing her estates.

Nor was Gustavus Adolphus so inconsolable that he could not marry. However, given how much time he spent abroad fighting wars, getting killed in the process, it sounds as though Ebba Brahe had the better bargain. A good few of her children survived to adulthood and, as her husband was also often away fighting, she was kept busy with their estates in Estonia and Sweden. And she had her *lusthus* in which to write. What she wrote, even my Swedish friends cannot say. Perhaps pastoral verse early on, giving way to more practical matters, agricultural prices, felling of timber, that sort of thing?

Of all this, the only element I wished to emulate was the way Ebba Brahe's *lusthus* is reflected in the water. Admittedly, my pond is not much bigger than her summerhouse, so there would be precious little water to do the reflecting. The whole idea may have been preposterous, but my hopes were high. I thought that the spoil Philip had dumped to make a higher terrace should be allowed some time to settle, then *lusthus* preparations could begin. Meanwhile, I sowed grass seed.

∾

Alas, sometime between one visit and the next, the pond emptied out. I could hardly believe it as I stood looking down at the thimbleful of water left in the bottom, with the Siberian irises now stuck far above. It was as though a plug had been pulled. For many visits after that I would scuffle about in the few inches of wet, weedy pond bottom, looking for any sign of where the water was draining.

At last, in the new part of the pond, I saw a slight twirl in the water surface. The twirl led to a stone, the stone led to the broken edge of a terracotta drainpipe. It was half filled with mud but with a good flow of water running into it. Then the water went underground until it emerged into the hand basin and so into the streamlet running down to the ditch.

When Philip had told me about the numerous terracotta drainpipes that he, in the course of his work, was wont to smash, I had winced at the thought of all that hard toil of previous generations being so easily undone. I had not, however, thought further about it. Now I wondered how the water still seemed to know its way. Maybe the excavation had interrupted an old line of pipes. Sure enough, poking through the upper bank was another broken pipe, with water dripping in from an angle different from Mr Scriven's inlet. Andrew had spoken of a herringbone pattern of drainage, and this angle seemed to confirm it. I decided to consult him about all this. I doubt if Ebba Brahe's management of her estates ever needed to descend to this level of detail.

∾

After Philip and his digger had cleared the thicket from Long Hill Orchard, the ground looked ravaged. The heat of those bramble bonfires had been enough to fire the clay underneath to the colour of flowerpots. Everywhere else was dark soil with long, black, tattered strands of bramble and a scattering of elder stumps. Andrew's plan was to sow the whole area with grass seed in the spring, then to 'mow out' the weeds when they came back through.

I could not help thinking that the ground, so rutted, squashed, strewn with woody rubbish, looked very unlike the illustrations in gardening books of soil ready for grass seed. By early spring, down by the new fence where the land had been clear for longer, there was already some greening-up going on, in its own fashion. I cleared a patch of this haphazard greenery, then raked and sowed grass seed in the approved manner. Sure enough, up came a neat green handkerchief.

When I was a child, Fisons, makers of chemical fertilizers, advertised their products by spelling out their name in fertilized emerald letters on the soft green of hilly pastureland. My fresh-sown handkerchief stood out just the same, so a friend called it the Putting Green. This did not prove that seeding the rough ground would not work, only that taking care with preparation did.

The trouble was that the Putting Green only covered about a thousandth of the area. *If seven maids with seven mops swept it for half a year . . . ?* Unlike the Carpenter, who only doubted, I well knew that the job of preparing all that ground by hand was beyond me. Ploughing seemed a possibility; Ted talked about attaching something behind his tractor, but it was not a subject in which I could interest Andrew. He merely said that he was ordering up a special seed mix suitable to the ground and that I should get the stumps removed, otherwise they would mess up the mower.

Still thinking of the ground, not the stumps, I reverted to the seven maids idea and asked a party of friends to come with rakes. It was by this time the spring of 2006, April Fool's Day, to be precise. Despite that we did well, getting most of the woody detritus piled and burnt. The tread of multiple boots may not have left a fine tilth, but the soil was at least raked, and did look more welcoming to grass seed than it had before. That left the stumps. Someone calling himself The Stump Buster was advertising his services in the local press. From the accompanying image, it looked as though he might arrive bouncing on springs.

The Stump Buster came on a beautiful late-spring morning, not bouncing but carrying a heavy grinder on a trailer. He was a gentle soul, the son of a farm labourer, who lived in the village of Spaxton, near Bridgwater. Spaxton once had quite a reputation, thanks to its Holy Man or, as we might be more likely to regard him, chronic abuser of women and young girls. The Rev. Henry Prince, one of those religious charismatics around whom the air gets overheated, established his 'Abode of Love', complete with 'Soul Brides', behind high walls in 1846. Undeterred by scandal (and his activities really were scandalous), he was allowed to continue in his ministry, or criminality, until his death.

'Nothing like that in Spaxton now,' said The Stump Buster, who was conducting a leisurely appraisal of the job. He liked my land, he liked it very much, he thought that he and his girlfriend would love just such a plot themselves. He rolled himself a cigarette and stood, admiring the view. While inwardly purring at this approval I did begin to wonder if the peace of the morning would ever be broken by the sound of stump-busting. All in good time it was, the angled blade of the grinder surging through the stumps below ground level with the motor whining, or snorting if asked to take on too much.

Once the stumps were gone the ground was as ready for grass seed as it was ever going to be. Andrew came with his sacks.

He is not usually one for handwork so I thought he would use a tractor, but he just slung a bag of seed over his shoulder and set about sprinkling, like a figure in a Courbet or Van Gogh.

∞

After the big clearance I could get close to several more old apple trees. One, which I used to call the Gatekeeper because it stood at the border between the Rollalong and the wilderness, fell down as soon as all the growth round it was gone. But it lives on, at least for a while, as the Fallen Gatekeeper, holding up two branches as miniature trees. Another grows above the pleasing hilly shoulder of land that was revealed by the clearance, and six more line the walk to the boundary ash.

Of those six old trees, the one at the beginning of the walk was hollow, with a globe of mistletoe at eye level looking like a Christmas decoration on the front door, and woodpecker holes further up. The middle ones were a tangle of collapsing branches. The three furthest were leggy as giraffes, holding their apples aloft as though laughing at the human far below. As with the other old trees, I wanted to restore or replace them with the same varieties before they died.

That might have been straightforward, if it had been easy to establish what those varieties were. But as things stood, I needed to get on with learning to graft. Little by little I had already been picking up hints, but reading and looking at diagrams only gets you so far. I wanted a practical demonstration.

That winter, there was a pruning and tree-maintenance morning at a nearby orchard, so I went along. It was a cold day. Out we stepped along the rows, each tree much like the last, till we came to some that had not already been pruned. None of the trees seemed to have much character, but I reproved myself for looking for any. This was a commercial orchard, after all, this is what Sir Thomas Browne means by regular ordination. I forgot to look for quincuncial planting.

The demonstration began, buds, spurs, last year's growth, light, air, etc. I kept trying to listen, but to me pruning has never seemed as simple, or as interesting, as its exponents maintain. Everyone else in the group found it very interesting and asked many questions. Crows flapped overhead, lower down some speedy little birds I could not recognize whizzed past. We moved on to some older trees, hearing about extendable loppers and the need to remove decaying wood or crossed branches. We were to remember the 3 Ds when judging which branches to remove: Dead, Diseased . . . what was the third one, Deviant, perhaps? The wind sharpened. I looked at my companions. Muffled up as they were in fleeces, waxed jackets, flying caps, padded trousers, hiking boots, few of them looked warm. At last it was time for coffee, indoors.

Our teacher, still wearing his fingerless gloves as he clasped his warm mug, was mobbed by questioners. When the crowd dwindled, I asked if he planned to tell us about grafting. 'No, what do you want to know?' 'How to do it.' 'It's very simple,' said he, before proceeding with a complicated account of scions, rootstocks, sharp knives, incisions, marryings-up of cambium layers, waterproof tape. 'I see,' I said, getting out a scrap of paper and trying to sketch two twigs in the sort of marriage he seemed to be proposing, 'is it like this?'

'Sort of,' he said, 'look, what you should do is to get hold of some rootstocks straight away and plant them. Go to Scott's of Merriott. Then find some good scions on your trees and stick them in the ground somewhere cold, so they'll be ready to graft in the spring. That's all you need to know at the moment.'

It was years since I had visited Scott's of Merriott. I feel lucky to have had occasion to do so again, a few times, before this old, well-loved nursery faltered, revived for a while, then shut. Scott's catalogues, with their cover drawings by Robin Tanner, their lucid descriptions and erudition, were of a sort to make an armchair gardener of almost anyone. As well as two lots of rootstocks I went on to buy several fruit trees from Scott's, at first two apples, a Reinette Ananas and a Tom Putt. I chose the Reinette Ananas because it has pretty, yellow-green fruit, tasting, to the willing imagination, of pineapple. The attraction of Tom Putt was its red fruit. How can an orchard be complete without red apples?

Tom Putt had a separate association for me. The catalogue entry reads: 'Tom Putt, once rector of Trent, near Sherborne. His namesake is a large red striped fruit', which took me straight back to my father. My father lived for some years near Sherborne, whence he liked to drive to Trent for the pleasure of the well-kept beer in the Rose and Crown, and the cordiality of the landlord. At that time I was always a passenger in the car, with little idea of how one village lay in relation to another. So more recently, on the way back from Yeovil, it had been a surprise to see the name Trent on a signpost. I turned off towards it.

A small place among trees, Trent seemed unchanged in forty years. Even the landlord was still there in the pub, although no longer behind the bar. He was sitting quietly, elegant, parchment-pale, with the withdrawn look of old age, but benign as ever. When I planted my Tom Putt, it went in with fond thoughts for both of them.

The rootstocks were in the ground. I had chosen to plant them in the cottage garden because that avoided having to protect them from nibblers. They could be moved later, if any of the grafts took. It was New Year's Day, 2007 when I walked round the wood trying to gather scions. Sir Thomas Browne had been little help with his observations on grafting, although a fine diversion. I would like to know if he tried any of his proposed experiments for 'conjoining plants of very different natures in parts, barks, lateness and precocities', and if so, what came of them. But I was a novice. Grafting rosemary upon ivy, almond upon willow, bramble upon gooseberry, or any of the numerous other combinations his open-mindedness suggested to him, sounded like a project for someone more competent and leisured than me. I only wanted to make descendants of the old apple trees before they were lost.

In the search for scions I knew what to look for: stems of fresh growth no thicker than a pencil, with good buds. But nothing that I could see was like that. Putting on new growth did not seem to be what the old trees were doing; it was more a case of a crabby, lichened holding-on, even up at the tops. I took some unpromising twigs and labelled them with a diligence that felt excessive, given their appearance. As instructed, I stuck them into a cold, north-facing spot of soil, so that their buds would not be tempted to *move* till late spring.

Near the wood I had often stopped to buy fruit from a stand outside a farmhouse, dropping the money into a pipe leading somewhere out of sight. Not only apples, but gooseberries, plums, pears, even juicy Black Hamburg grapes would appear on the stand, in priced bags, sometimes with cards saying that the grower was a member of the Fruit Committee of the Royal Horticultural Society. Various local people had told me about him, saying that for advice about fruit he was the man.

Usually I bought from the stand without seeing anybody, until one previous July day I had stopped for plums just as an elderly man appeared at the metal gate to the farmyard. I was greeted with great courtesy, then told that he was not the fruit-grower. He seemed to imply that he was really no one important. But the fruit-grower, I heard, was not only a very knowledgeable fruit-grower who would be sure to want to help me, but an extraordinary dancer as well. Then a somewhat younger-looking man joined him.

In the ensuing conversation, not all of which I understood, it appeared that I was being invited into the farmyard behind, to be shown some wonder. The fruit-grower went ahead, but I was detained to hear a little more praise of him. By the time I entered the yard, unaccompanied, it was empty. I looked around, wondering where to go. One door led down to a store-room, another hung open, showing a barn. As in a fairy tale, it was the third door I tried that was the right one. It did indeed open upon a surprising sight in the context of a farmyard: a perfect little dance studio, sprung floor, old-fashioned record player, glossy photographs, everything bright and orderly. The fruit-grower showed me round with pride. He had been a dance champion, now he was a teacher. He spoke in a soft, northern voice, saying one or two things that gave the impression that his early life might not have been so comfortable as his present circumstances.

Ballroom dancing I admire, but it is not something I know about. We used to foxtrot round the gravelled playground of my all girls' school trying to look sophisticated, but along came Chubby Checker doing the Twist, or rather our tennis coach imitating him, and the foxtrot dropped below our horizon. I felt I was making a poor response to being shown this gem of a studio.

Although the dancing fruit-grower did agree to show me how to graft, a hint of awkwardness had already set in. It was to attend all my dealings with him. My first blunder occurred when I called in to check something about the scions. It was winter, early snowdrops were in flower by the front door. I, dishevelled, had not expected to be invited in but was asked to sit in a beautiful drawing room with a pure-white rug. Shifting my feet, I saw that the rug was no longer pure-white. It is impossible to remove all trace of mud with a tissue and spit. The chagrin of that mud, the graciousness with which it was dismissed as unimportant, the snowdrops, are all that remain in my memory of that visit.

At Easter, arriving with the swallows, the fruit-grower came to the cottage garden with his grafting equipment: sharp knife, raffia, tub of sticky brown wax. He was displeased by the knobbly scions. When I apologized that they were the best I could find, that the trees did not appear to have new growth, he said I must prune them to promote it, but that as he was there, he would try. I watched as he made neat diagonal cuts to the rootstock and scion, then a little lip in the stock for the scion to snuggle down into and be held, even without the raffia. The raffia went on next, to make a tight join, then the wax to keep out the rain.

It was a mild morning, with sunshine coming and going and birds swooping in and out of the hedges. I was to try making the swift clean cut. I did try, but mine had ridges. Then I was to try being bolder with the knife. This time the cut was smooth enough, but scoop-shaped instead of straight . . . so many ways there are, of getting things wrong. We worked on till the grafts were done and labelled, although the fruit-grower remained pessimistic about them. He left me the rest of the tub of wax, for which, as indeed for everything, I was grateful.

It was only as he was leaving that I felt something was amiss, but not until he had gone did it strike me: perhaps he had expected to be paid. What a clot I felt, and still feel, not to have realized it in time and cleared things up, but instead I flurried off to the garden centre, bought some plants as a thank-you gift, and left them near his back door. Whether he found them, I did not hear. Thereafter what I had hoped might become a friendly relationship soon petered out.

The grafts failed, as predicted, although the rootstocks continued in fine health. Because of their height and frailty I did not prune the old trees into producing new growth, but three that had fallen over seemed to have taken their fall as a stimulus. By the time of my next winter search for scions, there were new shoots coming straight up from their leaning trunks. I repeated the process of gathering, labelling, heeling in and waiting.

The next spring, equipped with scions, grafting knife, wax and raffia, I prepared to have another go. The way the rootstocks had grown on, ignoring the failed grafts of the previous year, had produced some odd shapes. The knife was new but surprisingly blunt, the wax was cold and stiff. Once I had placed its tub in a bowl of hot water, it became too soft and runny. Only the raffia was just right, but these many defects seemed to lend me bravado. There is something to be said, after all, for not having an expert looking over one's shoulder.

Much to my pleasure, over that season and the next I did get some grafts to take. They formed small, rather ungainly maidens. Other trees that I had been putting into Long Hill Orchard were tucked round the edges of the open grassy space, into any available pocket of shelter. By the time the grafted trees were big enough to be moved the sheltered pockets were full, so the young maidens, *feathered maidens* by this stage, had to take their chance in the open. With Cyrus and his well-drilled armies still in mind, I tried to line them up with Ted's trees.

So far, although their progress is nothing to boast about, all but two of them are growing, putting forth some blossom, even setting an apple or two. Young trees should not be allowed to fruit before they have had time to establish themselves, but I felt that just one apple could do no harm, and would help with identification. Later, consulting Liz Copas's book, I concluded that one of the grafted trees is Broadleaf Jersey, 'a rather indifferent cider apple'. But it is the child of one of the old trees I want to preserve because they belong there, and also the child of my grafting. Like any parent, I see no indifference in it.

Butterflies on the
Buddleias

CHAPTER 7
Mowers, Hooves, Teeth

And since the lawless grass will oft invade
The neighb'ring Walks, repress th'aspiring Blade,
Suffer no Grass or rugged dirt t'impair
Your Smoother Paths . . .

JOHN EVELYN, SYLVA (BOOK IV)

AS SOON AS THE GRASS SEED was broadcast over the cleared ground of Long Hill Orchard, I was longing for it to grow. If I had been there every day it would have been like the watched kettle never boiling, but being away made it seem as though it had shot up overnight. From one visit to the next, a green pelt had transformed the dark, frowning soil. For a brief while it looked perfect, before the attendant weeds pulled themselves together and adjusted to the revolutionary possibilities. With more light and space than they had been offered for decades, what joy then to be alive, to flower, set seed and ride the wind, or edge outwards in ever-spreading growth. All to say, my new expanses of grass did not go unchallenged.

At that time a retired couple used to keep a table outside their bungalow, on which dahlias, tomatoes, cakes, marmalade would appear for sale, in order to fund their Council Tax. The garden at the front was plain and neat; the work that went into producing these things all happened backstage. On the opposite side of the lane a big field had been left uncultivated as part of the government Set Aside policy.

By chance I met and chatted with the dahlia-grower at his gate one afternoon in dry, late summer. As he was speaking, the old man's gaze roved over the Set Aside field, where acres of thistles had gone to seed. All of a sudden he raised his fist and started shaking it at the thistles, exclaiming that they were like the Germans advancing, they would soon be in his garden, how was he to keep them out when fools came up with an idea like Set Aside?

He was of an age perhaps to have had personal experience of the Germans advancing. I looked at the field with him and, sure enough, there they were, tall, grey, in massed ranks, all leaning forwards, aiming at his garden . . . but only armed with thistledown. Impressed by this encounter, I too tried to keep the 'enemy' at bay when it first arrived in my new grass, by gathering up and destroying the thistledown. The thistles advanced anyway, so quickly that I was puzzled as to how they were doing it.

Although acquiescent in the short term, I had not yet come to terms with the need for regular mowing. I was hoping for something more pastoral, quiet, green. In other words I was hoping for sheep, although not sheep of my own because you cannot keep livestock at a distance. I was hoping for someone else's sheep.

I knew that the higher fields nearby were designated as ancient downland, with orchids, harebells, blue butterflies and organically fed sheep brought in to graze among them. I also knew the sheep's owners, organic farmers who run a local farm shop, so I asked them if their sheep would like to eat my grass too. Although confident of their kindness and positive intent, I was still nervous when it came to showing the grass to them, because they are proper farmers.

However, it was not the grass itself that failed the inspection, it was the fact that the area would need electric fencing and there was not enough grass to make that worthwhile. I could not then afford fencing. The happy vision of all that nibbling, of dainty hooves, of contented bleating, faded away. But I did at least learn why the thistles were spreading despite having their seeds removed. Creeping Thistle was the answer.

∽

Mowing seemed inevitable, mowing with a petrol-driven ride-on mower. But there was one more possibility I wanted to consider, and that was mowing with a scythe. One or two friends of a greenish, concertina-playing bent had mentioned scything to me before. It had been a surprise to hear that scythes are still current, but I was soon put right about that, and told about terrain in Austria where the scythe is the only viable tool for haymaking. The idea that tough old parties up Alps are still scything because they have no alternative seemed only faint encouragement. Tolstoy found scything hard, and he was a big, tall man with something to prove. I had every reason to think I would do worse than him. But still, I did want to find out about scything.

As with so many aspects of my wood project, a slight lead revealed unexpected vistas. Far from being outdated, scything seems to have advocates and practitioners all over the place, competing, co-operating, trading, using their arcane vocabulary, scorning the rest of the petrol-driven world. I was intrigued by the possibility of taking scything holidays in Transylvania. As it happens, I have long harboured a fancy for Transylvania, because of Count Miklós Bánffy and his grand trilogy of novels about the decline of Hungary before the First World War. He had big estates and wrote about the Transylvanian countryside with a love and lyricism undimmed by the exasperation and despair he felt as the old Hungary unravelled. He finished his trilogy in the 1950s when his world was already lost, but the wild flowers and butterflies live on, thanks to a lack of modern agriculture.

Short, however, of travelling that far and enduring a scything holiday, I found much of interest at the Green Scythe Fair at Thorney, near Langport. This annual fair started in 2002, but my brother and I did not sample it till later. The entry fee was reduced for those who arrived by bicycle or horse, but we were not alone in parking a petrol-driven vehicle in a nearby field. From there, past a tethered horse cropping the grass under a tall poplar, we followed the sound of music, folkish but quite loud. It led towards a gathering of tents and stalls, set out with an air of theatricality to look like a street in the middle of the grass, populated by men in leather jerkins and women in colourful knitwear. The children were bouncing and sliding on hay bales, but the dogs had to be kept on leads. An old mobile pizzeria, looking cheerful, curvaceous and unroadworthy, was filling the air with oily, spicy smells.

At first we found anything but scythes among the stalls of books on how to make wattle-and-daub houses, of knitted and felt hats, leather belts, turned wooden bowls, boot brushes in the form of hedgehogs, wooden toadstools with thatched tops, old planes, saws, garden tools. Then we came to a sight that I found discouraging, a standing frame from which, like instruments of torture, hung five or six scythes. Their handles appeared to have been made from thick lengths of naturally curving wood, with knobbles, knots and all. Their long, curved blades looked so murderous that the idea of my being able to handle one of these things was suddenly revealed to me as absurd. 'Don't you ever go near that scythe!' an uncle of mine used to say to my cousins. I do not recall him saying it to me (maybe the scythe had gone by my time), but having looked at that array of scythes at the fair, I feel it would have been an easy instruction to obey.

However, there was a soft-spoken man sitting beneath the stand of scythes, working on a blade and looking the picture of peaceable industry. We asked him about the programme for the afternoon. He said that the chances to try using a scythe and the competition heats were over, but that we were in time to watch the finals. As we picked our way between guy ropes in the direction he indicated, we entered an area of the field where some patches of grass had already been cut.

We were not sure what to expect. I had pictured a row of people all scything together, as in *Anna Karenina*, the winner making faster progress than the rest. But there were very few people there, and no one who looked like a competitor. A couple of dogs, free and zigzagging despite the injunction about leads, were alone in looking as though they knew what they were doing. As the starting time came and went, there was a gradual gathering. Then, perhaps twenty minutes later, a man appeared carrying a scythe, and another with a clipboard. We crowded round.

Each competitor had a separate, taped-off allotment of grass to cut, one after another. They were timed as they worked and then there was a lull between each scything for some clipboard work, quality-control perhaps. My racier version might have made for a more exciting spectator sport. And yet it *was* interesting, to me at least. My brother's dog, a professional at picking up pheasants, looked on impassive.

What struck me was that cutting grass with a scythe is a very lengthy process. Here they were, the finalists, doing their best to get through a small patch as fast as possible, and yet even they seemed snail-slow. Maybe in Austria or Transylvania there are people bred up to the job who can do it quicker. Or maybe taking it steady is just how it's done, *time passes slowly up here in the mountains*, and so on. When we have used up every drop of fossil fuel, if we survive until then, we may be glad that this old skill has not been lost. But in the meantime, how easy it is to understand the lure of the machine.

Ted told me once that people new to Aller, *townies*, were making it hard for the man who mows the churchyard, because they wanted him to let some of the grass grow long. It used to be a straightforward job, keeping the whole place neat, but now he was confused, caught between differing ideas. This story Ted slid into one of our conversations about mowing, in the sideways, tactful way he often used to make a point, although in this case I was unsure what the point was. I was a townie, yes, with daft ideas, possibly, but I was at least trying to do something to maintain the land.

Other examples of Ted's indirect introductions had been easier to clarify. 'I was up your way the other day' had turned out to mean that he had been in a London hospital for a major heart operation. His 'she had a baby but she was never married' took more reflection on my part. What was so special about that, why was it repeated, and accompanied by such a significant look? After a while it trickled through to me. The old man in the remote cottage of whom we were speaking lived with his sister. It was the sister who, years ago, had had the baby . . . so had the brother been the father? That would fit in with that area's reputation, and perhaps with another story I had heard.

I was told that before the war, low intelligence in some of their patients had been so noticeable to a pair of local doctors that they had carried out some research. How, and to prove what, I did not hear, except that it connected isolated communities, inbreeding and low IQ. Then the war came, and with the war the Americans. New blood. When the doctors repeated their research after the war, hey presto, up had shot the IQs. This tale may not be reliable; I only retell it as a tangent to Ted's hints.

∽

As soon as Andrew undertook to mow the grass, he started trying to train me up to replace him. He hired an old red ride-on mower that he said was better for rough land than a new one would be, because its body was made of metal, not plastic. The circumstances in which this would be an advantage were not spelt out, but I could only imagine that they related to collisions or overturnings. But, he claimed, the whole process of working the mower was very easy and very safe.

I was to have a go. The engine was already running, it was an early evening in May 2007, the light soft, the air calm, Andrew and his sons were there to help. I was reluctant about having them as an audience, but really there was no excuse to put it off. I did want to learn, and liked the idea of buzzing about independently, keeping the place in trim.

We were not in the new spacious area, but surrounded by obstacles. Ahead of the stretch of uncut grass was a clump of elder trees, then the trickle taking water from the pond down to the ditch. Brambles grew on either side, with the beloved old apple, First Tree, to the rear.

The mower and I proceeded. Bumping forwards, then lowering the blade and feeling it engage with the grass was all right, even pleasing. Glancing backwards I could see that the grass was indeed being mown, and falling in a neat line. Dream-slow as this was, however, the elders were getting closer. I did not drive straight at them, but there was soon no room left for a gentle, continuous turn. If Andrew had mentioned the reverse gear I had not taken it in, but at least he had told me how to stop (an advance on the amateur instruction I once received about skiing).

So, as the bramble and elder loomed ever nearer, we executed a kind of arabesque before coming to what felt like a graceful halt, nose to nose with a wall of bramble. Was there a round of applause? There was kindly laughter.

It had been a very short lesson but I thought that that was enough for one evening, and clambered down. At such moments, how good, how stable the earth feels underfoot, and much more agreeable than the snow-covered manure heap in which my first ski run had ended. To call it a ski run is too grand. It was just a few moments of intense alarm, hurtling down a hillside behind a Swiss village. With me looking, or so it was said, as stiff as Queen Victoria.

Reflecting on that skiing moment, I now see how silly it was to have started without being able to stop, but I was more trustful then. It had been my once-upon-a-time husband who had set me off down that slope. He was a brilliant, attractive, but not altogether reliable young man.

∾

In terms of things looking in order in the wood, the big party I gave around this time was the high point. Andrew mowed and mowed and filled in rabbit holes beforehand. He ordered up a marquee and portaloos, he sorted the tricky question of where people were to park, his sons acted as stewards, his good looks brightened the eyes of some of the guests, and he cleared up afterwards. It was altogether a star performance.

But afterwards, the grass kept growing. Andrew recommended that I should buy the second-hand mower he had hired and said that his neighbour had to get rid of an old shed. He offered to put the shed up near the Rollalong, to house the mower. I agreed, although with some concern. The thing that I liked about my strimmer was that it was new, did not go wrong, and I could start it. The mower was far from new, it had put in years of service mowing a big lawn somewhere, before being sold to the contractor who had been hiring it out. Easy starting was not among its virtues. However, any new ride-on mower costs thousands, even those made of plastic.

The mower and shed arrived. It was a tight fit to get the mower through the door. Andrew would reverse in without difficulty but I could only go in forwards. It was my trying to back in, and braking suddenly, that caused the mower to *throw a belt* for the first time.

A mower has a surprising number of belts, and mine was very given to throwing them. If one of its wheels lurched into even a small grass-disguised scoop in the ground, nothing as deep as a rabbit hole, one or other of the belts would snap and there we were, stuck. The first time it happened Andrew was with me. He tipped the mower on its side, tugged out the torn belt and showed me the frayed ends. It was not my fault, he said, it looked old and ready to go. I was to take the old belt into Dave Locke's and get a replacement. Meanwhile he tipped the mower back upright and pushed it into the shed, two procedures I could not manage, although there were to be many occasions on which I wished that I could.

I was already familiar with Dave Locke, a man who looks to the manner born wearing blue overalls and holding an oily rag. Having some time ago sold the family shop and yard (F. J. Locke, established 1899, as it says on his van), he continued his metal and machinery work in part of a farmyard. Customers would park in between two barns, one filled with lathes, the other, intermittently, with calves. Never yet have I heard Dave say he could not mend or recondition something, from a push-mower to a metal dome. On his side of the yard all sorts of metal objects would pile up awaiting attention, wrought-iron benches, gates, railings, a cupola from the top of a civic building, the cauldron from a disused laundry.

Over my ride-on mower period I was a frequent visitor, and Dave came quite often to the wood. At first the mower needed some work to make it start more easily, then there was all the throwing of belts. No longer could it be said that the belts were breaking because they were old; they had all been renewed but still they broke. I was beginning to despair, not of the mower itself, which was a game old thing, but of the conjunction of it, me and the rough ground. As Ted was once moved to remark, watching me on that mower was 'better than looking at the marathon'.

I asked Dave to find a smaller mower, thinking I could trim round the fruit trees while Andrew could use the big one. Dave is very tall. To him pulling the long starter rope of the mower he chose was simple, but it was not for me. Only sometimes could I get that mower started, and after such effort that it felt like time to stop for a cup of tea. I asked if he could shorten the rope, but he thought that was a bad idea. My brother, Andrew and Dave all encouraged me to keep on with the mowing but I was feeling more and more resistant. I would pass the mower shed without looking at it. The mowing itself and the riding around were fun; it was the attendant breakdowns that were dispiriting.

The last time I went out on the big mower I had persuaded myself to give it another go. It started easily, we reversed out of the shed without trouble; it really seemed as though the power of positive thought was at work. But after a stretch I looked back, expecting to see a strip of cut grass. There was a ribbon about four inches wide of cut grass, with all the rest just flattened. I raised the blade, lowered it, tried a second time. The same. It was too much. I put the mower back in the shed and never tried again.

I forget how Dave accounted for that last failing, but it was not so serious that it meant the end of the mower's days. To my pleased surprise, he said that a young man who was just starting out as a contractor would like to buy it. When he came and collected both the ride-on and the mower with the long starting rope, I watched their departure with a mixture of regret and relief.

After that I began looking about at the delightful mown paths winding through waving grassy meads that have of late become so popular in big gardens and parks. Would delightful mown paths winding through waving coarse weeds be equally poetic? Seized with this thought, I experimented with shearing a path from the Rollalong to a circular patch that I had designated the Butterfly Garden. Shearing a path is laborious, but not impossibly so. I kept up the practice for a few years. To my partial eye the grass of this path became much more delightful than that to either side of it. But I do not want always to have to cut it by hand.

❧

The idea of a butterfly garden arose from the question of mowing. The mowing I asked Andrew to do was not fine lawn-mowing, more an occasional swipe to keep the ground open, sometimes infrequent enough to let the thistles and burdock flower. This flowering was clearly much to the insects' liking. They seemed to favour one particular warm and central area of the grass as it sloped up above Ted's orchard, so I chose that for their garden.

Thinking of possible plants for this sanctuary brought back to mind the whole question of categories, of what is or is not suitable to grow. There are many distinctions to be made: between plants that are native or not native to Britain, those considered wild or cultivated, those that do or do not like wet clay soil, or those with natural defences against creatures. Also, there are the plants I happen to like or dislike, or those that prompt memories or associations. Having started out thinking only of trees, the fact that chance gave me as much orchard and woodland edge as woodland means that what I am doing is, in the roughest sense, a form of gardening.

'I know what this is,' declared a recent visitor, 'it's a forest garden.' I am not sure that he was right. Forest gardens, if I have understood the term, involve careful calculation about the combination of under-storey, middle-storey and canopy plants, while all that I do is consider of any particular plant, will this fit in or is it too gardeny? For instance, weeping willow and cork-screw willow look fine in among the wild crack willow and the red-stemmed one from my cousin's farm. But I walked around with a pot of the handsome grass *Miscanthus sinensis*, trying it here, trying it there, but everywhere it looked uncomfortable, like a smart guest at a raffish party.

If all the creatures shared the strict views that some people hold about avoiding non-native plants, I might take more notice. But they don't. In particular, I am thinking of buddleia, more precisely, *Buddleia davidii*. This is the one that seeds itself so well, that sprang up in bombsites and continues to flourish in railway sidings and wasteland. It was brought here from China in about 1890. It liked what it found, so is often dismissed as a common weed.

I had not thought of growing buddleia until happening to notice a wild one on top of a wall, part of the building site that was around Arsenal's Emirates Stadium in London. This buddleia had very long, trailing flower heads, far longer than normal. I looked up nurseries specializing in buddleias, and found that Longstock Park Nursery in Hampshire, not far off my route to Somerset, has a National Collection of them. Hoping that the long, trailing one would be of interest, I contacted them and took a sample to show.

Two men met me, one the buddleia expert. He was scornful of my trailing offering, calling it an ugly great thing, and could barely be persuaded to look at it before leading me off to see proper ones. It happened to be a sunny July day. As we approached, the double line of buddleias was almost enveloped in a great dance of butterflies, butterflies so thick in the air that you had almost to bat them away. There were tortoiseshells, cabbage whites, peacocks but mainly thousands upon thousands of painted ladies. There had been a report on the news about an 'effusion' of painted ladies arriving from France, an arresting thought in itself. Clearly, some members of that effusion knew about this National Collection of Buddleias.

Surprised as I had been to have my attempted contribution to buddleia knowledge so swept aside, to be among those butterflies made up for it. I half listened as my guide discoursed on

plant-breeding and the importance of deadheading while decid-
ing that, invasive foreigners or no, buddleias would be welcome
in my domain. Back at the nursery I chose some, including one
named after a butterfly, Adonis blue.

The other man was at the till. He gave the impression of
having felt sorry for the way my trailing buddleia had met with
such dismissal, saying that he had never seen one like it. He
also asked if I had ever visited the Longstock Water Gardens.
Which is how I came to enjoy a private viewing of a beautiful
place, and to sit in the summerhouse that John Spedan Lewis, of
the department store, built in the 1950s for the enjoyment of his
semi-retirement. Into this thatched retreat he had had a telephone
fitted, a state-of-the-art installation allowing him to be with his
water lilies without losing touch with his business partnership.

Before this buddleia excursion I had already been trying to
learn about and encourage my local butterflies. In high summer
out I would traipse, with director's chair and butterfly books,
to see what I could see, and project some well-meaning med-
dling. Before coming up with the idea of a circular sanctuary,
I was aware of feeling exposed, sitting there in the middle of
open grass. The thought of a ring of thistles and nettles, in the
middle of which I could sit secluded, began to appeal. Secluded
from what? Nothing really, it is not rational, it just feels more
comfortable to sit near a tree, or within some sort of enclosure
than out in the open. Inside the thistle ring, so the fantasy ran,
would be neatly kept grass, with crocus, lavender, rosemary and
other plants the insects like. And, now I had seen that host of
painted ladies, buddleias too.

How pleasing it would be to report that all of this has come
into being. The truth is, it has in part. But as the summer passes,
the thistly stockade becomes a drunken-looking affair, knit
together by bindweed and cleavers, held up by burdock in some

places, in others lurching to the ground. As a *hortus conclusus*, it lacks conviction. However, it is indeed visited by bees, moths, butterflies, dragonflies. There must be other visitors too, as the lavenders and rosemary were soon nibbled to death.

Foreign import or no, I think the most successful addition is that of the buddleias. Admittedly, they have not yet been so mobbed that I have had to wave butterflies aside. (The only time I have known that happen was when, one particular late summer, hundreds of red admirals were flitting about and feeding on the fallen apples and plums.) But even without being mobbed, the buddleias are a big attraction to tortoiseshells, peacocks, fritillaries, whites, tiger moths, painted ladies, commas, hoverflies. Meadow browns tend to keep to the grasses and thistles, as do various blues that I struggle to identify, and the little moths and flies for which I do not even try to find names.

On sunny August days, trying not to feel spurned by the plenteous insect life outside the chosen circle, I settle down within it to leaf through the books and revisit information that I had imagined was committed to memory . . . is that a small copper, a gatekeeper, a speckled wood, a marbled white? What is that caterpillar eating the buddleia leaves with something of the air of Billy Bunter, natty in white with yellow and black spots? Mullein moth seems to be the answer. The book warns that I am unlikely ever to see the moth. But, given that I have not graduated to the night-time outings of dedicated moth-hunters, complete with lamps and traps, I see few moths anyway. That sort of venture is something to look forward to.

Every so often, as I sit in the sun up come the clouds, at which most of my quarry twinkles out of sight. Only the meadow browns keep going as though nothing had happened. When the sun comes out again the other butterflies are back in an instant. I neither see them hide, nor see where they hide, nor do I see them emerge. It is like a conjuring trick.

In London I consult an old butterfly book, with no publication date but with an Art Nouveau design embossed on the cover, so probably published in about 1900. The authors make clear in their preface that they consider their index of English names an advance in accessibility, although no one now would accuse them of talking down. The fact is, this book is not an easy read. But for me it has several endearing features, including my mother's maiden name written on the fly-leaf in faded ink, the coloured illustrations and the names of moths in the English index . . . *Shining Chimney Sweep, Short-cloak Carpet, Shoulder-striped Wainscot, Shuttle-shaped Dart . . . Footman, Fortified Carpet, Four-dotted Footman, Fox Moth, Foxglove Pug, Frosted Green.* A striking thing about this book compared with the modern ones I keep in the Rollalong is the greater number of entries in its index.

∾

Whether or not they are native to these shores, I would like various flowers to naturalize themselves so that they come up every year without further intervention. According to this wish, the year would start with snowdrops and hellebore, move on to crocus, wood anemones, primrose, narcissus, bluebells, campion, camassia and snake's head fritillaries, then irises, moon daisies, knapweed, yarrow and other desirable wild flowers, with only a token showing of the nettle, dock, bindweed fraternity. In the autumn, just as thoughts of flowers are receding, little cyclamen would appear.

Of all these lovable flowers, there is not one I have not tried to grow. Snowdrops, narcissus and a bold, adventurous geranium, Wargrave Pink, that I brought by mistake along with a beech sapling, are the ones that look most confident of having made themselves at home. Much of this planting starts off within enclosures round the fruit trees, marked off by logs to save them from being mown. When first made, these enclosures look neat and orderly but they soon lose any municipal air, so quick is the regrowth of grass and weeds.

Old-fashioned varieties of narcissus had become an object of desire to me before I bought the wood, prompted by a visit to the garden of a house built in the 1920s. Looking at the narcissus there brought straight back to my mind the stands of tall, slim, wispy ones in my aunt's garden. Her house, too, had been built around that time and the narcissi in the two gardens must have been planted soon after. We called the tall, slim ones narcissi and the shorter yellow ones daffodils, which is not correct, but is a usage that persists.

My aunt's narcissi came up every year. I was not aware of having taken much notice of them until this more recent sighting returned to me their elegance, their soft colours and scents, their air of fragility. To see them again was to wish to grow them. Luckily, so did other people. By this time, old-fashioned narcissus varieties were already being collected and discussed.

In one instance, this collecting was by chance. It so happens that Ted's son Philip, being a digger-driver and a motorcycling enthusiast, sometimes has occasion to dump heaps of soil in Ted's orchard, to make bumps for his son and other boys to ride over. In this way interesting things arrive, including daffodil and snowdrop bulbs, hellebores, cowslips, poppy seed, fossils, even the stone cherub that Philip let me have to adorn the approach to the Rollalong. Although it is not at all my business to be keeping an eye on these things, I do find them irresistible, which is how I came to notice that some of the daffodils growing in random clumps looked as if they were of old varieties.

Old fashioned Narcissus

At first I was restrained, doing nothing but admire these beauties from afar. From a conversation I had with Ted about his daffodils, I sensed that that was all I should be doing. But as time passed and the motorbike-riding did no good at all to some of the clumps, I could resist no longer. I knew that Ron Scamp of Falmouth, doyen of daffodil-growers, would have a stand at the Bath Spring Show, so I picked some specimens to show him.

Ron Scamp turned out to be a friendly man, who looked at the flowers with care. One, he said, was probably White Lady and an old warhorse. But the other . . . near the orange-coloured cup the soft-yellow petals were edged with orange, looking as though it had been painted in watercolour with thin pennants of the orange running from cup to petal. This flower won more of Ron's attention. It was, he thought, a Leedsii, probably from the 1860s, and not one he already had in his collection.

I told Ron about the orchard that was not mine, and the motorbikes, and asked if he would like me to try to get some bulbs. I knew that he understood the delicacy of the situation, the absolute importance of territorial boundaries, from the way he said, 'Well . . .' We agreed that, so long as I could get them without giving offence, two bulbs would be enough. With circumspection, the deed was done and the bulbs wrapped and posted. And just two of them were enough. The last time I spoke to Ron he said he now had about a hundred of them, an illustration of how much it helps to know what you are doing.

Later on, as the motorbiking further wore down the daffodil clumps and Ted's continuing ill health kept him away from his orchard, I asked his wife, Doreen, if I could rescue a few more. Which is how I come to have some of the special ones growing just inside our dividing fence. I placed them there with the thought that it is really one continuous space, that I was not appropriating them very far.

This thought about continuous space has also occurred, of late, wet years, to the cows. When it rains so much that the fence posts wobble it is no trouble to the cows to push them over and walk in. I love the sight of them in Ted's orchard but, so far, have never seen more than a stray calf in mine. It is their great, heavy footprints that give them away afterwards. That, their cowpats, and what would appear to be a fondness for low-growing apples.

❧

One plant that I have imagined growing in the open ground below the grafted apple trees is the peony. Not an obvious choice for an orchard, indeed probably a bad one from the fitting-in point of view, but one with connections to this area. Repeated visits to 'Peony Valley' at Kelway's Nurseries lie behind this idea. Kelway's of Langport, a survivor from the heyday of Victorian nursery gardening, is one of the town's few claims to international fame (being the birthplace of the economist and writer Walter Bagehot is another). James Kelway, head gardener, son of a head gardener, established his nursery in 1851 and prospered for the rest of the century, making his name famous for gladioli, irises, a surprising number of other flowers as well, but most lastingly for peonies. Or paeonies, as they were known.

Peace and plenty favour gardening, not least plenty of cheap labour, so the first half of the twentieth century brought hard times to the nursery trade. But the firm kept going, managing to project an impression of glamour through its stylish catalogues even if backstage things were not running so smoothly. Between the wars, to visit Kelway's Peony Valley in June became a fashionable outing, as talked up by the garden writer and early radio broadcaster Marion Cran.

That use of the word 'valley' is, it seems to me, an example of what happens to people's perceptions when they live in a flat landscape. Any little variation causes excitement. True, there is a stream running through the peony field so there must be a bit of slope, but hardly enough to notice. However, Peony Valley it is. Photographs from the 1930s show it looking very neat, with rows and rows of peonies growing on either side of a gravelled path.

Time has done away with the neatness, but the long, rough rows of untrammelled plants still look beautiful, growing up through grass, splaying out their great blooms in all directions, the whole field of them better for not being mixed up with other plants. With so many whites and pinks shading through to deepest purple-red, the only background they need is the darker green of their leaves, then the greens of grass and trees.

It is that evidence of the toughness of peonies and how well they look in a field that makes me wonder about planting them. The effusive Mrs Cran was right to say of the Peony Valley, 'When once you have been there you come out different; you have been in an enchanted place and you are restless and unsatisfied until you can grow some of those beautiful flowers for yourself, to make a new memory of that day when you first saw the valley.' Quite so, or quite nearly so, since I question the idea of making memories on purpose.

One of the reasons I have not yet done anything about this peony idea is that although those old stock plants in Kelway's Peony Valley are holding their own in rough grass (or were until recently), they would not have been planted like that. It would take a lot of labour on my land to give new plants the conditions they would need to get established. And then, they might look out of place.

∽

Thinking about mowing had become a part of my life. In terms of machinery, there was still one more card to play. I was aware that there are petrol-driven mowers that start with a switch rather than a rope. Dave Locke was cautious, saying that the switches can go wrong, and as these mowers are more recent there are fewer second-hand ones. However, to have a look, I was to visit a showroom in Wincanton.

To go from Dave's shadowy barn of a workshop, the gloom often enlivened by sparks from the welding, to the showroom's bright lights and colours was like fast-forwarding from the Industrial Revolution to some uncertain time where the present and future overlap. In the showroom, flanked by rows of mowers as colourful as children's toys, there was a central plinth. In pride of place upon this plinth a small, grub-like robot was trapped inside a large astro-turfed aquarium, forever nosing across the green until it approached the sides or corners, at which it would back off at an angle and resume its endless roving.

This, as I understood it, was the future of mowing, the walls of the aquarium representing the obstacles, the bushes, borders, steps, which a robot mower would know to avoid while cutting a lawn. It was one of those sights that are hard to stop watching, but at the same time pitiful.

The robots may be on the march but it might be a while before a robot mower would suit my purpose, and even longer before I would suit a robot. I asked the salesman for a walk-behind motor mower that never failed to start when switched on, that was light and easy to handle but strong enough to deal with weeds and uneven ground as well as grass. The salesman said that you could have some of those things from one model, some from another, but not all at once. But, he continued, all these models are self-propelling.

Self-propelling does not mean what it suggests. I already knew that, hence the wish for a small machine. It was disconcerting how enormous were the models on display, how even the 'small' ones seemed to have puffed up from the simple, scraggy things they used to be into great lawn galleons. It was as though Morris Minors had mutated, bloating into four-wheel-drives. I did not leave the showroom quite empty-handed, taking a light, battery-powered strimmer for the paths. But the perfect mower still awaits discovery.

For all the irreplaceability of machinery, I continue to think of hooves and teeth. Every year since Ted's decline I have watched with anxiety for the arrival of the cattle in his orchard, because I love them being there and am never sure if the arrangement with the local farmer will hold. They tend to come twice, once in the spring when the calves are young, then in late autumn when they have all grown thick, hairy coats. Most of them are black and white, some are brown and white, deep rusty-brown or buff-coloured. A few have fine, curly horns.

Although I have wished that the cows could come and eat my grass, and they have wished the same, their occasional unscheduled visits have made it clear that having them in is not an unmixed good. This awareness, along with an email from Andrew, has brought me back to the idea of sheep. Rob the organic farmer's sheep in particular.

It was not a complete surprise to receive an exasperated message from Andrew concerning rabbit holes and damage to his mower and his son's ankle, but it acted as a stimulus. By this point I could think about paying for fencing, so a plan to enclose the grassy parts, leaving the woody areas free for the wild animals, began to form. Sheep, with their 'golden hoof', might then, as they were famed for doing in medieval times, bring the land into better heart. Fencing and gates may not be a decorative addition, but if they usher in an era of better management, I will accept that.

Much discussion, and waiting, has formed part of this scheme. The question of what the sheep will and will not eat came up. 'They don't discriminate much,' Rob warned, 'they'll probably eat things you don't want them to.' I already fortify the young trees against the rabbits and deer, so thought that that might be all right. But what about these undiscriminating eaters encountering plants that are bad for them?

There is a tall, feathery plant with blotchy stems, like a bigger, less pretty version of cow parsley. It arrived of its own accord, but as it had settled round the edges I had not taken much notice until thinking of the sheep. To find out what it was came as a shock. Hemlock, such a fell-sounding plant, right there in the wood? It is not just there, but widespread along the roadsides. Similarly, the ill-kept verges are a seedbed for ragwort. That noxious weed I already knew to uproot; now hemlock has joined in. The Internet offers stories of hapless foragers dying of hemlock-root stew and cattle poisoned when hemlock roots are exposed by ditching work. So I approach all this with high seriousness, rubber gloves and well-tied disposal bags.

Naturally, as it is their defence, many of the other wild plants are poisonous as well. Too many to try to control or, says Rob, to be worth worrying about. So the sheep need to use their common sense and not eat briony, arum, honeysuckle or buttercup. I was delighted to hear that they will eat bramble leaves, and be harmlessly nourished by them.

Now that Nick, the fencer, has done his work, the sheep have been in, once in spring, once in autumn. In no time they made themselves at home, pounding out their follow-my-leader sheep tracks to link together the two open areas on offer to them. It was soon clear that they favour the hilly shoulder of land. From the way in which the grass and certain wild flowers grow there, but not elsewhere on the four acres, I had already speculated that that shoulder might be an outcrop of the limestone underlying the ridge further up. Maybe the sheep think so too.

Various details of this sheep scheme are now becoming clearer. One, that I was wrong to think that the same chicken-wire tree guards that deter deer and rabbits would be enough to hold back sheep. Sheep are heavier, and quite capable of barging down chicken wire in pursuit of one or two choice-looking shoots of apple or lime. Another detail is that the fence is annoying, to me and doubtless to all the other animals.

However, even if this has not so far shown itself to be the perfect labour-saving scheme, and the grass has yet to be transformed into a delightful weedless sward, I live in hope. The fencing does give a look of husbandry, which has a certain appeal. And, or so I try to comfort myself, it is not in the nature of this project to yield instant results.

the crows nesting in the
ash trees

CHAPTER 8
The Banks of Green Willow

The willow tree will twist
And the willow tree will twine . . .

'I Sowed the Seeds of Love',
folk song collected by Cecil Sharp
in Hambridge, Somerset, 1903

H AMBRIDGE, A STRAGGLE OF A VILLAGE a few miles from Langport, may not look like the epicentre of anything, but it was. It was where Cecil Sharp, ardent collector of folk song and dance, really got started. He was visiting his friend, Charles Marson, Christian Socialist, perpetual curate, who was the local clergyman.

Hambridge Church and vicarage jut up out of the flat land, separated by a short stretch of road. Not far behind one side of the road, emanating the quiet, green, passed-over air of lost enterprise, lies the Westport Canal. After the effort and expense of building it, the canal company made money for only a short while. In 1903, when Cecil Sharp visited Hambridge, twenty-five years had passed since the company had been wound up. Agriculture, too, was doing badly. The area would not have been looking prosperous, but he found it rich in another way. It was not the first time he had been there, but it was this visit that set ablaze his already kindled interest in folk song.

At that time Charles Marson had been living among his parishioners for several years, seeking to understand their tough, constrained lives with the same sympathy that had endeared him to the poor Londoners with whom he had previously worked. Around Hambridge he knew that there were singers who could remember songs long out of fashion, with melodies they had learnt by ear and words that might or might not have been printed on broadsides and sold at fairs for the last three centuries or so. To hear his gardener, John England, singing 'The Seeds of Love' may not have surprised him, but Cecil Sharp was thrilled.

'Living song' Sharp termed it, meaning a song being sung as part of everyday life, to entertain the singer as he scythed the grass rather than a song that had already been pinned down, collected, printed, performed. He was eager to hear and conserve more songs before the singers should become forgetful or die. Sharp was not the first collector of folk song, but he pitched into the pursuit with fresh energy and enthusiasm.

Word of mouth was the way to find singers. A new lead would have Sharp and Marson bicycling along the lanes to Muchelney, Long Load, Drayton, Langport, Bridgwater in search of the cottages of willow-workers, gardeners, farm labourers, shirt-makers. Some received their visitors with a mixture of pleasure and amusement, some with shyness or suspicion, but many were willing to sing. Sharp listened to the mournful, modal tunes, noting them down, while Marson concentrated on the words. The co-operation between them was fruitful, until misunderstanding wormed a way in and spoilt it.

Bicycling along the lanes in the twenty-first century, it is and is not easy to get a sense of how the countryside would have appeared to those two eager collectors. They might recognize the elm and hawthorn hedgerows, the occasional oaks and willows, the billowing cow parsley and wide, breezy skies. But the fields are much emptier of people than they would have known them. 'The people are going away fast, and in a couple of generations there will be neither songs nor singers in the silent fields,' wrote Charles Marson in the preface to the song book he published with Sharp.

Marson was right about the absence of people singing, but not about the silence. Total silence would be alarming, but where there are hedgerows the birds still sing, and the intermittent rumpus of farm machinery, road traffic and helicopters from the airbase at Yeovilton at least prove there is life about. And there are still cows kept outside, and sometimes, along the lane past Muchelney Ham to Long Load, a series of bulls, each majestic but usually isolated in a field of his own. One winter, when their land was flooded and I was out admiring the expanses of water, I came across two of them, no longer separate but taking refuge together where the fields slope up. Hay had been tossed in under an oak tree along the lane hedge and they were sharing it, rubbing cheeks and shoulders in a companionable way.

The singer I was most drawn to learning about was Mrs Overd of Langport, because the cottage tucked in next to my garden in Langport is called Overds Cottage. When I read that Mrs Overd had sung 'The Banks of Green Willow' to Cecil Sharp in 1904, I wondered if he had visited her there. As I soon learnt, this was wrong. Someone called Overd must once have lived there, but Mrs Overd the singer lived nearer the river.

Anyway, she was out at the pub when Sharp came calling. Accounts of their meeting dwell on the hearty greeting this stout lady in her late sixties gave Cecil Sharp when he enquired for her outside the pub, dancing him round and calling him her beau. He was more than twenty years younger than her. When she sang to him he was impressed by her 'great dramatic fervour'.

I wanted to find out if any of Mrs Overd's family were still living in Langport. Shirley Nicholas, I was told at the newsagents, was a direct descendant and the one to contact. Shirley Nicholas, née Overd, may not have whirled me round in a dancing greeting as her great-grandmother had Cecil Sharp, but there was a warmth and friendliness in her response that made me think it might be a family trait. 'Well yes,' said Shirley later, 'we do like people.'

The family, she told me, had never lost sight of the fact that Emma Overd had been a singer. However, they had not taken much notice either, until various outsiders started showing an interest. Shirley's father had loved his grandmother and liked to speak of her, but 'You don't listen much when you're young, do you?' Yes, singing did still run in the family.

Emma Overd could write, unlike her farm labourer husband ('They were very poor, you know, really poor'), but she kept the words of the songs in her head. Although she must have learnt them, Shirley assumes, from older members of the family, they have not been passed down.

Even if Emma Overd's songs have not been sung by every succeeding generation of her family, Linda, Shirley's daughter, has taken up singing some of them again. In the mellow quiet of Fivehead Church, with only Shirley and me for audience, she sang, unaccompanied. The songs conjured up the customary scenes of love, separation, betrayal: a daughter with a baby left outside in the cold, a fine lady off with the gypsies, a young man robbed, a servant girl seduced, sailors leaving their sweethearts behind. Linda's voice is warm, untrained, musical . . . for all we know, like her great-great-grandmother's.

I had read that Emma Overd lived in Knapps Lane, in between the river and the railway at Westover, Langport, and had gone looking for anything resembling the row of cottages in front of which Cecil Sharp took photographs of her. It was puzzling; no railway any more, nothing called Knapps Lane, and the only possible cottages smart and unrecognizable. 'No, they've gone,' Shirley told me afterwards, 'only a bit of wall left.' She said there had been a willow-stripping shed down there with a boiler to soften the bark, where Emma had worked. I found none of all this, although the man who now owns the land mentioned that he had come across a lot of bricks littered about in the middle of the field, so perhaps they were the remains of the willow-stripping works.

Even if there were no traces of Emma Overd, I did come across an unexpected sight. There, nestling among grasses and burdock on the other side of the railway bridge, was a company of old three-wheeler cars, Robin Reliants. Rusty, flimsy, some with wheels, some without, placed in a ragged oval as though at a convention between themselves, they looked as if this may not have been meant to be their graveyard, but might be becoming so.

There is an old photo hanging in the nearby office of Langport Motors, showing almost the precise spot where the Robin Reliants stood becalmed, but presenting a very different face. In the photo that ground is the platform of Westover Station, a train is appearing under the bridge, men in Army uniform are drawn up in ranks, presumably about to board the train. It would have taken them down to the south coast.

Thence, where were they bound . . . to other graveyards, perhaps, in France, in Turkey? The men in the second rank look very small. Maybe it was late in the war and they were boys, allowed to lie about their age.

The trains that had taken away the work of the Westport Canal, and then carried men away from the farms, stopped running under that bridge decades ago, leaving it to be blocked with metal containers. Whoever owns the Robin Reliants will not agree, but to me their presence was in tune with the abandoned railway, the vanished platforms and withy-stripping sheds, the lost cottages where Mrs Overd, along with other women, once lived and sang to lighten the hardship of their lives.

When I was at school and made to sing folk songs or dance 'Strip the Willow', I never thought about where these things had come from, or why we were singing or dancing them. Now, realizing that Cecil Sharp had had an influence on our childhoods, I began to wonder about him and the tendency of his work. Thus one morning I found myself in the Vaughan Williams Memorial Library of Cecil Sharp House, in London.

Scorpions nest everywhere, especially among the opinionated, so it should not have been a surprise to come across records of a few of them sequestered in that quiet spot. Sharp, it seems, was loved or loathed in his own time for his inspirational energy or for his tendency to dominate. Later the loathing centred on his methods, the way he could be seen to have patronized or exploited the rural poor, and to have turned his back on their urban fellows.

My own feeling towards him is of neither love nor loathing, but of ambivalence. I feel glad that he listened to the likes of Emma Overd, that he took photographs of them and noted their songs. But as for having to skip about to the accompaniment of monotonous tunes in a school hall . . . for any contribution that he may have made to the backwards-looking constraint that overhung my schooldays, the constant disapproval of anything contemporary or fashionable, for that I cannot thank him.

∾

Willows are still grown as a crop around Langport, as osiers to be cut each year, but Ted once told me that there had been a big change in the way the old crack willow trees lining the waterways are valued. When the pollardings were still worth something, people used to argue over who owned particular trees, but now that maintaining them costs rather than earns money, no one wants to own them. So the willows fall about, taking root on both sides of a ditch that may divide one property from another, and getting on in their own dishevelled ways. Along the roads it is different; there they still get a short-back-and-sides every so often.

When I planted the fiery-stemmed willows grown from slips from my cousin's farm, it was only with the hope that some day, far in the future, their winter colour would stand out from a distance. But that was to underestimate how willows love wet land. Within only a few years they were already tall and bright enough to be seen from far away. If you know the precise place to look up to from your train window, as you flash by between Castle Cary and Taunton in winter, there you will see a momentary blaze of orange among the leafless trees. Not that people tend to look out of train windows any more, but maybe some winter walker, glancing up from the business of choosing where next to tread, will be pleased to see it. And even if no one else notices that hopeful flare of colour, I do, and love it, and point it out relentlessly.

Further along the River Parrett, past Aller Drove and on to Stathe, there have been more winter visitors, thanks to the arrival of the great cranes. The cranes were raised from eggs at the bird sanctuary at Slimbridge in 2009, then brought to the Levels to establish themselves in the wild. But how were young cranes, nurtured by humans, to learn to fly? There are some wonderfully comic pictures of people decked out in what appear to be grey bin-liners, flapping their arms and running. Heaven knows what the crane chicks made of them, but they obliged; they lifted off and took to the air.

Many local people have seen the cranes flying, but I have yet to do so. It is always exciting when the heavy beat of wings announces that swans are flying over, but to be fossicking about at the wood and look up to see a flight of cranes . . . that would be special. Meanwhile, I have looked through a telescope to watch them feeding out on the moor. A less than poetic sight it was, a bunch of dull-coloured, dowager-like forms paddling about on their long legs, perhaps not altogether delighted by the Somerset Levels in February.

I could see them thanks to the presence of a well-equipped pair of birdwatchers from London. I had heard that the cranes were being fed by the river, so had turned up imagining they would be right there in full view, like ducks on a pond. It was not like that. There were a few cars parked on a scrape of gravel by the lane, a footbridge over the mud-coloured river, but nothing else to be seen by the naked eye except flat land, grey sky and a few earnest-looking people.

The couple from London, who were as kind as they were well accoutred, dressed from head to toe in dark green and with a treasury of tripods, telescopes, binoculars and other, to me, nameless gadgetry, knew the precise direction in which to look. A help, that, in a wide, sedgy landscape only punctuated by the occasional huddle of windbent trees, fencing, electricity lines, or the reedy suggestion of a ditch. They had already set up their tripod and telescope, and let me take turns to watch. After about half an hour of squinting at the cranes picking about, thirty-five of them my companions reckoned, and with no sign of them flying, I had had enough.

It was quite different with the kindly couple, however. They were proper birdwatchers who, with a look of calm, bright anticipation, were settling in for the second of their three-day visit to the Levels. They were staying locally, had arrived in the light the previous day, gone out for supper, then spent a long time in the dark, twisting lanes trying to find their way back. I sympathized with that. Even in full summery daylight those lowland lanes have a deceiving way with them, of promising one destination or offering a glimpse of a landmark on one hand, then, as though following another scent, lighting off in another direction. After detouring past many views of cows, ditches, piles of old tyres and skies, the place originally sought, or the church tower that stood out so clearly, will reappear, but on the opposite side to the one expected. This looping about, not as arbitrary as it sounds, is to do with water. Everything is, around there.

∾

The wish to encourage tourists is strong among those in charge of the local economy, now that farming employs next to nobody. For some years Langport billed itself as 'The Heart of the Levels' and leaflets carried the phrase 'Share the Secret', accompanied by drawings of walkers, cyclists, birds, otters, dragonflies.

My wood is not on any official path, but still, some sharing of its secrets seems to go on. One Sunday morning I arrived to the sound of a chainsaw and found an amiable young boy with a dump of equipment on the ground. He explained that he was the son of the caravan site-owner and that his elder brother and friend were making a motorbike trail through the woods. With pride he showed me a looping track they had cut through brushwood and ivy, to link with the main slope where, I saw straight away, they had removed one of my newly planted beech trees. When I said that the land we were standing on was mine and that their motorbike trail could not come through it he looked taken aback. His elder bother came and expressed equal surprise. I showed them the boundary bank as far as it is traceable and agreed to send a copy of the plan. After they had gone I dragged branches to mark where their trail had to stop and re-erected the wire guard round the destroyed young beech, in case it might sprout again (which it did not).

I went home heavy-hearted. I could understand that to ride motorbikes up and down that woody slope would be fun, but even if the trail kept to their side the noise would not. Disliking the idea of a dispute, I nevertheless contacted the planning department to find out about motorbike trails. How glad I was to hear that they should only be used for fourteen days a year.

Ted's son Philip loved trail-riding. He had his son Jamie on a bike around Ted's orchard when Jamie was still tiny. One afternoon Ted and I had stood watching them, little helmeted Jamie bumping up and down round the trees. The sight put Ted in mind of the pastimes of his own youth, when less was laid on for children. He and his friends, he said, used to train up jackdaw squabs as pets. Each boy had his own jackdaw on his shoulder as he walked to school. They would part with them at the school gate, the jackdaws would get on with whatever they wanted to do, but then at home-time there they would be, waiting for their boys. I loved the image of the shoulder-riding jackdaws, and chimed in with the 'lost golden age/children today' conversation with Ted.

Given that watching the no-longer-tiny Jamie and his friends careering around Ted's orchard on bikes can be a pleasure, I tried, without success, to reconcile myself to the idea of the woodland trail. In the event, however, what had seemed a looming problem faded away. There was no acknowledgement of my letter but I have never heard motorbikes, and only once saw tyre marks coming down the slope. I replaced the beech with a walnut. I have thought of Robert Frost's neighbour's line, 'Good fences make good neighbours.' It sounds right, but only if the good fence can run along an agreed boundary. In this instance, a good fence might make worse neighbours.

I had heard some talk of a local coven of witches making black magic. So the day I arrived to find a curious emplacement in the hazel wood, consisting of chairs and watering cans taken from under the Rollalong, with logs arranged into a sort of altar or high jump, I recoiled. A ritual site? I inched towards it, in dread of the blood-red dashes visible on the ground. They turned out to be flakes of paint from one of the chairs, but I was still nervous until spotting Hubba Bubba sweet wrappers littered about. Although sweet-eating witches might well choose ones called Hubba Bubba, it seemed more likely that my visitors were children from the caravan site, playing some inscrutable game of their own. Even so, there was a disconcerting air to their arrangements. It took me a while before I could pick up the wrappers, take back the chairs and watering cans, replace the logs on the pile and breathe more easily.

Once I found two bundles of dead crows tied with orange baler twine and thrown in through the hedgerow. With their

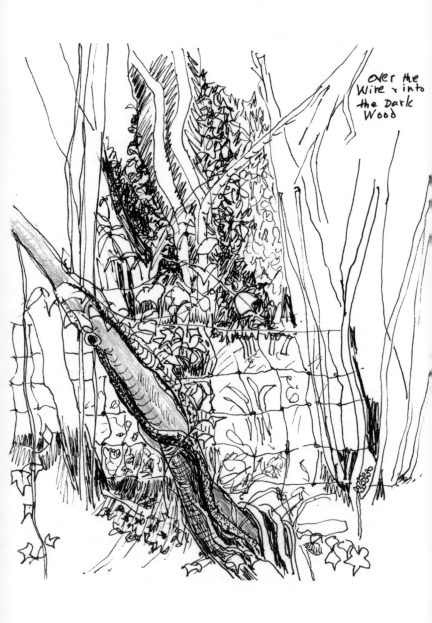

over the
Wire + into
the Dark
Wood

sunken bodies beneath their dull, roughed-up feathers, their pitiful legs and claws, they were horribly changed from the look of sleek insouciance they have in life. The next day a man with a gun was pacing down the side of the wood, dressed in combat gear. I was pleased my brother was with me, but the man was mild enough, the expression on his fleshy face neutral in a way that suggested generations of practice in not having a clue. He agreed to remove the dead crows. Naturally, he knew nothing of the spent cartridges.

Many of the people passing through my land are either lost adventuring down the slope from the caravan site or trying to walk back up to it from the road below. On finding themselves straying through an interim domain they tend to respond either with delighted surprise or with truculence. A teenaged boy from Yeovil, shepherding his younger siblings through the nettles, won my heart by looking round and saying softly, 'it's so beautiful . . .', but a middle-aged woman with knapsack and silent husband did the reverse. They had walked up from the road. As soon as she saw me she stumped up complaining about the thickness of the undergrowth and how the way was not clear. I pointed out that it was not a way, but that they could climb over the wire above the hazel wood and join a track further up.

'It certainly is a footpath,' she declared, 'there's a stile down at the bottom.' There is no stile and it is not a footpath, but, unwilling to argue whether black is white, I showed them where the animals have made an opening in the old stock fencing through to the higher wood, pleased to keep to myself what a ripping, stinging struggle awaited them. Throughout this exchange the man kept his head down. In my last glimpse of him he ducked lower to avoid a hanging curtain of ivy, stepped over the wire and followed the woman into the half-light of the ash wood. Into the *selva oscura* with them, thought I.

❧

If I have mixed feelings about the uninvited human visitors, I do sometimes recall that, for the natural wood-dwellers, I am one too. Unless it is completely dark when I arrive from London, I love to have a first idle walk around, seeing how things are. On that initial walk up the track, the degree of scuttling off, squawking, streaking away, clapping of wings on the part of the residents is almost always greater than it is on the following days. I get the impression that the creatures, in full possession during my absence, become more circumspect when I am in the vicinity. They do not go far away, often appearing on subsequent days, but the place feels a fraction less wild than on that first approach.

After I have left again, when gas bottle and steps are put away in the Rollalong and all is shuttered up, how long does it take for the wildlife to notice? I suspect not long. In the same uncanny way that dogs and cats are able to detect the imminent arrival of their humans, so human departure may also be perceptible. Hunters, field naturalists, wildlife photographers will surely know about this.

I may be an intruder, but some of the residents quickly accommodated themselves, if not to me, to the Rollalong. The space underneath it, a dryish place in a damp world, is favoured by a variety of them. A rusty-red, round bundle of fur was asleep at the bottom of a small log bucket when I came across it. It slept on soundly as I took care replacing the logs above it, making me think *dormouse*. But looking at illustrations later, I came to think *vole*. Some other provident character sometimes makes itself mossy, curtained shelters inside the hollow ends of the Rollalong's metal chassis, but I never see it. In lucky years there may be a neat exit hole, but a rude scattering of the moss curtain can tell a different story.

A friend's dog, a big, close-haired, lovable mongrel, once got very excited under the Rollalong, sniffing, scuffling the ground. What a fool I was to imagine I knew better than him, to think there could be nothing of interest there among the chair legs, firewood, plant pots, ladders. More scuffling, then out shot one, two, three, four little rabbits, cute as Easter bunnies, only running for their lives. In the consequent affray my friend was on the dog's side, I was on the rabbits'. There were no fatalities, but feelings were ruffled all round. It was, with hindsight, one of the last scenes of an on-and-off, mainly off, love affair that had started when the dog-owner and I were eighteen. So there it is; some hopeless loves expire on stage at La Scala, some end with fur flying under a Rollalong.

The dog only threatened them once, but the rabbits in the wood are always at risk. A scream from a young rabbit was the cause of my seeing a thin streak of an animal, wild as wild. It was like a ferocious, grey fur glove hurling itself through the air. I think it had brown points to its paws, a stoat maybe. I was close enough to interfere, hoping to save the rabbit. Its attacker sped away, unfed, while the rabbit convulsed and died. I left the body where it lay, hoping it might get eaten later, thus not have died in vain. But there it remained, a waste, a reproach to one who has never accepted *red in tooth and claw*. I want the wood to be the Holy Mountain, with no guns and the lion lying down with the lamb, but it refuses to exempt itself from the real world.

The second time I was there when a similar scene was enacted I steeled myself not to intervene . . . but it was a bigger rabbit on this occasion and, as the screams went on and on, I wished I had. Over time I have had to listen to quite a few heart-rending shrieks, wondering why the victims cry out when there can be no hope of rescue. Is it emotion, are mice, shrews, voles, rabbits, small birds expressing terror? Anthropomorphism, yes, but the distinction between people and the other living beings has never felt at all absolute to me.

The only other time I intervened on hearing screams nearby I did succeed, if that is the word, in saving a jay from the grip of a buzzard. It was on the edge of the wheat field. The buzzard, often to be seen sailing above the wood, exchanging mournful-sounding cries with one or two other buzzards, had come right down low and must have been about to dispatch the jay when I approached. Startled, it let go and flew off, leaving the jay to tidy itself up for a moment, shrug off a loose feather or two and carry on its life. Or so I hope.

Despite having several kinds of predator, and sporadic returns of myxomatosis, the rabbits' resilience and industry are impressive. Old records mention warrens along the ridge at Wearne, making it seem likely that rabbits have been living locally for hundreds of years, under control at first, but wild for much longer. 'My' ones are always busy with new excavations, throwing up with their slight feet great mounds of the clay soil I find hard to work with a fork or spade, making holes in ground I have designated as paths and showing a curious liking for the area below the pond. In very wet winters the entrances to their burrows may brim with water, but still they keep to that area.

Animals may live in the wood but they also die there. Mostly it is only a bone, tooth, hoof or skull I find, but a few times the air has been filled with a smell so pungent and rotten it could only be from a substantial body. Once I followed such a smell out into the field, where a handsome, well-grown fox with a gaping bullet wound lay dead among the wheat. Who had shot it? Who leaves spent cartridges in the wood? These are questions to which I have never found the answer.

When the smaller animals get killed there is, for obvious reasons, very little left of them afterwards. There may be a scattering of rabbit fur or pigeon feathers, but nothing much. With the bigger ones it is different. I hate finding the carcases of deer, foxes, badgers. It does not happen often, but each time is a shock. Usually, the first intimation is the smell.

On one occasion the smell was very bad but its source was hard to find. It seemed to come in wafts, first from this thicket, then from that. Friends were due to visit soon, many new to the wood. The thought of their being greeted by such a stench lent urgency to the search, but pacing back and forth, peering and sniffing, it took a long time to spot the body of a big deer.

Clearing brambles for a closer look revealed a startling sight. It was summer, the deer was lying on its side, its ruptured cavernous gut alive with maggots, hundreds and hundreds of them in a great rippling mass. Along every bone, especially where its ribs curved to form a sort of proscenium arch, more maggots queued as though in a multi-flyover traffic jam. The smell was so foul I wondered what to do. The ground was dry, there was no possibility of digging a grave, nor would it be at all easy to fetch bags of compost from the garden centre to cover the body. With the party still a week away, I decided to wait and see.

There was something gruesomely attractive about those maggots. Wherever I was in the wood, I kept being drawn back for a look. The day after I had found them they were still undulating in their thousands, with the smell just as bad. Then rain fell long and heavily that second night. The following morning I approached the dead deer with the same dread, but the scene was quite different. The grey rib cavern had been washed clean out, leaving scarcely a maggot. Tissue was still stretched between some of the bones and a few live maggots were hanging on, in so precarious a way that it was hard not to feel sorry for them, survivors of the deluge. But they and the rain had done good work, leaving the bones almost bare and the smell quite gone. All I had to do was replace the brushwood that had been such an effective curtain before, and hope that other creatures would not, as they sometimes do, drag the body about.

Since owning the wood I have found several dead deer. They may have died of disease, old age, have crept up wounded after collisions with cars, or have been shot. Andrew says they have been shot, that poachers go around 'lamping', driving an off-road truck with lamps rigged to an overhead bar, dazzling the deer into becoming easy targets. I was doubtful that the poachers would have driven up on to my close-grown land, until finding wide diamond-patterned tyre tracks from a vehicle that must have swung in through the gateless entrance. At some point, perhaps deaths later, there would have been a grass-wrenching three-point turn before it swung out again. When Andrew confirmed that he had no such tyres, that it was sure to be poachers, I speculated about having a gate put in. But he said, 'Waste of money, they'll smash it down.'

In truth, at that time I did not really want a gate. More recently, the advent of the sheep has made one necessary, but back then, apart from Ted and Philip's fencing along our shared boundary, the extent of my land was either sketchily marked or not marked at all. I liked this softness, the blending in with the rest of the landscape, the way the animals could make their paths through without any hindrance. Looking from the bottom of the track it is possible to see with some precision where the old orchard ended and the wood began, because of the difference in height between elder and ash, but that clarity is quite lost to anyone standing close up. The sheep enclosure has compromised some of this seamlessness, but not all of it.

∾

The pond lived on, more as a deep puddle than a pond. In very wet weather it would fill up, but in very hot weather, true to Mrs Scrivens's pronouncement, it never ran dry. There were frogs, dragonflies and plenty of other creatures getting on with their lives, unperturbed that the pond leaked. But I was perturbed.

Once those broken pipes and the outflow of water had come to light, something, sometime, had to be done. And that *sometime* swiftly became *now*, with the approach of the big party aforementioned. Andrew came and unearthed the run of pipes into which the water was flowing from the pond, smashed them and crushed them once and for all, then battened the earth down on top.

Again the pond filled in so promising a manner that, unbeknownst to me, he put in a number of young carp. He then told me about them, saying that they might as well take their chance, he needed to get rid of them because he bred carp and these were not bright or colourful enough. I was doubtful, not knowing how well the pond would hold or how well its smaller inhabitants would take this influx. But, being incapable of not feeling for the under-carp, I was glad these rejects were reprieved.

For a short while, the pond did hold. My friends came, musicians played on the site of the proposed summerhouse, somewhat surrounded by somewhat clear water. All verged, fleetingly, on perfection. But a few weeks later, out leaked the water again, leaving it about knee-high. This second time was less of a surprise than the first, but I worried about the carp. Hidden by watercress and other weeds, it was hard to catch sight of them.

The heron, however, knew the carp were there. Having been disturbed from its attentive pose by the pond, it flew up among the ash trees. There it spent some time, alighting on one branch after another, as though thinking of moving in with the crows. It seemed to me rather slow to realize that it was not welcome, or maybe it was unsure how to get away, tossing about in the air with crows darting and cawing all around.

As time has gone on, there have been many more crows, nesting and conversing up in the ash trees. By evening when they start coming home they have a great deal to say to each other, drowning out the voices of the smaller birds. There may be an occasional hush, making it seem as though they have settled down, but then one will let out another caw and the racket starts up again.

Despite the heron, one carp did live on in the shallow water of the pond, at least for some years. The last time I glimpsed a charcoal and dull-orange flash, it seemed to have grown a spine and be looking formidable, but that was a while ago. The carp grew and the number of dragonflies declined, but the two things may not be connected. After a spate of cold and wet winters, it might not be fair to blame the carp. The number of bees and butterflies has declined too, but no one would try to pin that on the carp.

I would like to know what to blame for the way the pond leaks. Andrew blames the rabbits for their tunnels, but speaks of waiting for the clay to 'plim' or possibly 'plimb' up, that is, plug the leaks of its own accord. After prolonged rain, when the rate of water flowing in exceeds the rate leaking out, it fills for a brief, tantalizing moment, at which I stand on the bank, willing the clay to plim. But the water, as I imagine, remembers the way it always flowed in the time of the terracotta drainpipes, and takes no notice of smashed pipes, battened-down earth or plimming in its hurry to get down to the river.

To line the pond is an obvious, although not straightforward, possibility that I have always kept in abeyance. This is in part because liner is usually laid on bare earth, not underneath a foot of busy, lively water. One sort of weed after another has vied to take over that modest volume: watercress, fool's watercress, a khaki-coloured mat-former with the texture of pan-scourers, mint, sedge, reeds, while I, in borrowed waders, occasionally attempt to hold the ring between them. Any rakeful of weed comes up glistening with water shrimps and other small invertebrates struggling to get back underwater. Sometimes, fat beetle larvae turn up and, once or twice, the hint of a water vole.

Ratty, of *The Wind in the Willows*, was a water vole, and his kind has been becoming scarce. If I am right that the solid-feeling body that once thudded against my submerged leg was Ratty, and that the holes in the bank are his, I would not like to seal them off with butyl liner. Also, after the last upheaval, the water took years before clouds of evil-looking stuff stopped blooming up from below. It may not be deep, but the water is at least clear again.

Meanwhile, the terrace of spoil, supposedly a level, grassy sitting place above a wild-flower bank, has slip-slid itself back into the profile of the original slope. Of all the wild flowers I have introduced there, knapweed, moon daisies, campion and yarrow have flourished, moving themselves in the process from

Knapweed & Sedge
at the Edge of the Pond

the bank I chose for them to the site for the summerhouse and the bank below it. Whether I ever get that *lusthus* built remains to be seen.

∾

If I had kept to my original intention of only growing woodland or specimen noble trees, the need to maintain the grass would diminish as the trees grew and cut out the light. But that simpler idea had flown straight away with the discovery of the old apple trees. Now that the young trees were starting to bear fruit, another question was becoming more insistent: what to do with the apples?

Ted used to sell his to a cider-maker who came to collect them, but his is a five-acre orchard of cider-apple trees, including the desirable Kingston Black and Morgan Sweet. Even for them, the cider-maker did not always find it worthwhile to come. I only have a few, of which several are cookers and eaters. The options were to give them away, to sell them, to process them in some manner or to leave them on the ground to get eaten or rot. The giving and the selling worked to an extent, as did the leaving on the ground, but none was satisfactory. I soon learnt how very little money growers receive for raw foodstuffs. All those jams with frilly tops and fancy labels began to make sense.

I tried making apple jam, which looked and tasted dull. Apple chutney was better, but made the kitchen smell for months. At last, the answer suggested itself – apple juice. Of one thing I was sure: I did not want to do the juicing myself. Wooden hand presses look beguiling in advertisements, but after the hard work of pressing there is more to do. As a cut apple discolours and later rots, so does its juice. To keep its colour, apple juice needs citric acid. To last, it must be pasteurized and bottled. When, in 2008, I heard that some cider-makers offer to do this work for a small sum, I was soon making enquiries. The first two said no, but the third, Hecks Farmhouse Cider of Street, Somerset, treated my queries as though I hardly needed to ask; of course I could bring over some apples when they were ready.

The barn and the yard of Hecks Cider, set among streets of newish houses, look like an outpost from an earlier time. There is no farmhouse, nor any fields, but as one swings in through the high gates, suburbia is left outside and the sweet-sour smell of apples takes over. Pomace, the leavings from the apple press that the cows love, lies in a fragrant heap by the gate, there are stacks of boxes with stencilled names, most from the West Country but some from Kent, Worcestershire, Herefordshire. Barrels, bottles and produce are on display in the barn used as a farm shop, with the apple press itself just beyond. It is not a traditional press with great screws, but modern, metal, low to the ground. Nissen huts, or buildings in that style, stand at the back of the yard. They are part of the operation, but not a part open to the gaze of the casual bringer of apples. A little white dog with freckled ears busies herself here and there, with only a few moments to spare the visitor.

I was nervous the first year, picking up the juice after it had been pressed. The apples had produced enough to fill forty bottles, but it might taste sour. If so, what to do with forty bottles of sour juice, all done up nicely with blue sealed tops? I took them away, putting off tasting till well out of sight. Then, in a layby, I untwisted the lid and took a sniff. It smelt good, but can one detect sourness by sniffing?

At last daring to taste, I was elated at how good it was; not just all right, but delicious, fresh, subtle, without the insistent sweetness bred into more recent apple varieties. How proud I felt of those old trees, and of the young ones of old varieties coming along to keep them company.

Picking the apples, grading them, carrying them along to Hecks each year, then distributing the juice among a select clientele has not turned me into a businesswoman. But how much better do I now appreciate the work of our small food producers, and know that it is unreasonable to expect good food to be cheap.

Cows by the River Panett

CHAPTER 9

Across the Moor

With hey, ho, the wind and the rain,

. . .

For the rain it raineth every day.

WILLIAM SHAKESPEARE,
TWELFTH NIGHT

IT IS NOT TRUE THAT THE rain rains every day, but in
wet winters on the Somerset Levels, with the rivers rising
and engineers making calculations about time and tide, it
can feel that way. Singing 'hey, ho' in the face of all that water
might be fine for a fish, an eel or a Shakespearean fool, but that
is not how the engineers see it. For more than a thousand years,
they have been working to control the water.

For the last half-century or so, these efforts have succeeded
in keeping the floods out of Langport. Before that, people living
near the river could expect the occasional flood. My cottage,
like most old buildings there, had flagstones laid direct on the
earth to allow the water to seep away, while pre-war photographs show people boating down the street. In the wet winter

of 2013–14 it looked as though they might be doing so again, but it never quite came to that.

Langport enjoyed its heyday in the eighteenth and early nineteenth centuries. There are lively memorials in the church, breathing confidence as they laud bankers and entrepreneurs, all to a man public-spirited, charitable and good. The town was a port, linked by the tidal River Parrett to the Bristol Channel. All the usual accoutrements of ports were there: wharves, boat yards, pubs, brothels, slums, warehouses, customs house. Despite being in the middle of the Somerset countryside, you could book a sea passage from Langport to America.

I was unaware of any connection between my family and the town until my brother Martin mentioned a slight one. He remembered, when young, visiting Langport with our dad, accompanying him on a call to an old acquaintance. Martin was unsure where this acquaintance had lived. Then one afternoon we were out on The Hill, the area furthest in all senses from my cottage and the former port. As we passed some cedars at the gateway to a gracious house he recognized it as the place he had once visited, more than fifty years before.

My father was old-school enough not to arrange visits; he simply turned up, expecting hospitality. That was the way things had worked before everyone had telephones, and for him it still worked. I had been on such outings with him, so it is easy to picture the scene: comfortable old furniture, stuffed pike in glass case, one-bar electric fire. *The Times* would be put courteously aside and refreshment hastily assembled, perhaps by an unseen hand. The talk would be of roads, directions, weather, politics, most of them going to the dogs.

On this occasion, my brother said, the conversation had strayed beyond those subjects. Unusually for my father, it had gone back to the First World War, in which both he and his host had served. Martin was then not long out of school, the same sort of age these two now-elderly men would have been in 1914. He ventured to say that he would never know how well he would have acquitted himself, in their shoes. Such an innocent, youthful remark; how could it cause offence? But the two veterans rounded on him in energetic unison, saying that he was not to put himself in their place, not to think about it, he was to be glad that he did not know, grateful for an easier time than they had had . . . My brother was taken aback at this unexpected heat.

It is odd how thoughts attach themselves to places. Now if I walk past the gates to that house, those two, my father and his companion, spring to mind. In all probability they had both been carrying the bitterness of their experiences all their postwar lives, without saying much about it. Then a chance remark, from youth to age, had been enough to stir it up. After my brother told me of their outburst, their emotion seemed to take up a tenuous lodging around that place.

Langport, as the dismissive 1907 guidebook admitted, has seen some history. It does not, day to day, feel much haunted by it, except by the ghosts of former enterprise, the stone gateposts to the old cattle market, the railway buildings, gantries, weigh-bridges. One enterprise that is not at all lost, however, is that of the water engineers. Along the ways I walk between Langport and the wood are many traces of their continuing task.

Although for convenience I more often drive than walk to the wood, the distance on foot across the moor is shorter, only a mile or so. It would be less as the crow flies, but the pedestrian crow is soon hampered by water, in the form of ditches, or rhynes, as they are called. Approaching across a field, you can get close up to a rhyne before realizing how much too deep and wide it is to cross, as those luckless seventeenth-century Royalists discovered after the Battle of Langport. So the route has to allow some indirectness to take advantage of the droves, the unmetalled tracks bridging the rhynes that allow the farmers to reach their fields.

There is a choice of two ways from the cottage to the wood, both starting from the end of the garden, which leads on to the moor at the back. There, immediately, the first ditch presents itself. I was led to understand that this paltry passage of water, never in my hearing dignified by the term rhyne, had once been a canal, and part of a complex endeavour. The plan had been to join the Bristol Channel all the way across country to the English Channel by means of a navigable waterway, part river, part canal. That the ditch had played a part in this story did not look probable.

My later reading about the waterway confirms that the ditch and the canal were not the same thing. The canal, which was necessary because barges could not pass under the river bridge, came off the river a short way downstream. It proceeded through the middle of the town, emerging to link up with the river on the other side.

Work on the local section of the waterway, called the Ivelchester and Langport Navigation, started in 1836. It was not very successful. First, as is usual, there were geological setbacks and money problems, followed by a brief period when things more or less worked. Then the railways stole away the trade. Much later, the canal across the moor and through the town was mostly filled in but a stump is still there, with duck-weed, hamburger packaging and brambles across its surface; an undistinguished end for a player in a grand scheme.

We riparian owners, as my neighbours and I have been called in relation to our ditch, have a varied array of footbridges over which to walk from our gardens on to the moor. Mine had rotted away, and the bulk of a collapsing willow was taking up the last section of the garden. Peter, the younger of my brothers, was for several years a great help in the wood and the cottage garden, despite being mortally ill. Fuelled by steroids, the clean sweep was his forte. But he was also a sceptic. Dismissing my piecemeal approach as farcical, he never really believed that I would get the willow pollarded or a new bridge built from the garden to the moor.

With Peter's clean sweeping and my tendency to leave things be, as cultivators we did not always see eye to eye. So I cannot say that every moment we spent together in the last few years of his life was in perfect harmony. But still, I very much bless the wood and the cottage garden for having brought us far more together, often in company with our older brother, sister-in-law and cousin, than we had been for decades.

I did not get the end of the garden opened up, the willow pollarded and the bridge built before Peter died in 2010. Now that those things are done, I often think of him as I open the gate and cross the bridge.

Once you are out on the moor, the river is only a minute's walk away to the left, but invisible until you climb the embankment. Invisible, that is, unless it happens to be flooding over in a shining, roaring mass. But usually it is further towards Aller that the engineers allow the water to spill over, surging down day and night till the fields disappear from view, leaving only a few trees to stand up as markers in the flood.

In general, the river lies low, allowing both my ways to the wood to start alongside it. The water often has wavelets ruffling the surface, making it appear to be flowing away from the sea.

Certainly it used to be tidal, hence Langport's history as a port. But as a swimmer I have never felt the incoming tide, only a strong pull downstream. There may be too much silt now for the tide to come up, leaving only the wind to create the illusion of a counter-flow.

Until 2006, a puzzling piece of engineering soon came into view along the riverbank. There is an island with a former lock-keeper's cottage. The derelict remains of something, unrecognizable either as a lock or a sluice, appeared just above water level. It was a large iron grid, reaching across from the island almost to the near bank. Moorhens skittered about on it, Isambard Kingdom Brunel was said to have designed it, and it did not seem to be doing any harm. But then, in the very year of Brunel's bicentenary, this relic vanished, removed, as I heard, for health and safety reasons.

However, there are plenty more examples of engineering to be seen from that path, most of them to do with water. Trains hare by between London and Cornwall, or dawdle along if they are carrying freight, held aloft from the soggy ground by a dark-purple brick viaduct of ten arches on one side, an iron girder bridge spanning the river, then two more arches on the western side. Telephone lines straddle the moor, with showy discs to warn the swans not to fly into them.

On the far side of the river stands a sewage works, with young conifers, including cedars, in front. Beyond them lies the sky to the west. Some day, if those cedars get to full size, they will be a fine sight against the sunset.

∽

The walker passes under the dark, dripping railway bridge to enter what feels like a different place. To the left, light and air, as with a bend in the river the horizon is suddenly much further off. The flat landscape opens up towards the west, often with the wind whipping clouds across the spacious sky.

Beyond the bridge is a big scoop in the ground, with willows in every stage of collapse and regrowth and the soil much poached by the hooves of cattle. To the right is a busy area of waterways. It is at this point of the walk that the two main routes diverge. The less discursive one is along the river.

For most months of the year, cows or bullocks occupy the fields on both sides of the Parrett, black-and-white ones to the north, grey-brown and creamy ones to the south. There are always some birds, gulls, crows, cormorants in the sky, with dropped mussel shells on the path. Ducks and moorhens fluster about by the banks. For a few summers there were kingfishers, but they seem to have come and gone.

Ahead, in the far distance, lie the Quantock Hills. In the near distance is an installation called Monk's Leaze Clyce, through which some of the water is diverted, roaring and foaming, into a man-made relief river. Clyce is another word for sluice. In the immediate foreground are often dogs and their owners, out for a walk. One misty night when it was almost dark I heard a man comforting his wary, growling dog, saying that the strange thing approaching was only a cow. When I turned out not to be a cow, the dog seemed touchingly pleased.

Further along the path there is a choice: to keep going by the river, or to turn away up a drove with little birds chattering and swooping among the hawthorns, sometimes a heron or an egret, or tortoiseshell butterflies on the flowering mint beside the rhyne. Along there was an old, rusty, bent and sinuous field gate that I used to like, but now all the gates are galvanized.

Staying by the river leads up to the clyce. Built of concrete in the 1960s, Monkleaze Clyce looks suitably plain and functional, in form like a carwash. But there is yet something of a thrill to stand beside it looking down, seeing and hearing the force of the water as it falls and seethes in the sluice. This is the point at which I need to turn away from the river to walk up past the hidden lake belonging to the local angling club.

Even in leafless winter you can see nothing of this lake, only the surrounding fence, ditch and bushes, with heavy padlocks, chains and 'Keep Out' notices defending the gates. Sometimes the gate across the pathway is also chained up. As I have often had to climb over that gate and then walk past all the stern notices, the anglers' exclusive arrangements had been working upon my curiosity.

For years the lake's defences remained impenetrable, but then came my opportunity. Maintenance to the fence must have been afoot, because some of it had been replaced by crash barriers, not all in perfect alignment. Checking that there were no cars parked by the entrance, in I slipped through a narrow gap, making my circumspect way along a path towards the lake.

What had I expected? Something of magical beauty, a jewel withheld from common sight? It turned out to be just a small lake surrounded by trees, with tight diagonal lines stretched above the whole surface detracting from any limpid gleam it may have had. I puzzled about those lines, wondering if they were yet another ruse against intruders, before thinking that the intruder, in this case, was probably the heron.

Soon after this adventure I got into conversation with a man from the Drainage Board, who was out to see how well the work of the previous summer was standing up to the first heavy rains. They had been strengthening the sloping ground down which floodwater would cascade into the relief river. This was autumn 2013, before it was yet clear how serious the flooding would become. So, with no air of urgency, he showed me the sheet of water flowing easily over the reinforcing mesh, commenting that it was a pity the grass growing through the mesh had not had time to establish better roots. In hindsight, it seems unlikely that grass roots, however firm, would have withstood the trial they were about to undergo.

We then started to discuss the anglers' lake, which lies a field's length down from the relief river. I asked if he knew why it was so defended, what was it the anglers feared? He laughed, remarking that anglers always like to keep themselves to themselves, but that the trouble could be poachers, that he had an idea there might be valuable old carp in that lake.

Valuable old carp . . . did that mean the carp were forever being caught, unhooked, then thrown back in, that the survivors would need to have developed a *here we go again* resignation? Also, what had happened to them in the floods; had their lake become part of the wider sea? The chance of meeting a talkative angler to whom to address these questions has not yet arisen.

The engineers are often tinkering along that stretch of river. It seems that they may have changed their minds about which section of bank to allow the river to flood over, because it used to be further along. From the wood I could see the falling sheet of water through binoculars, a distant, unapproachable Niagara.

On a wintry day in an earlier flood year, the roar of the overflowing river had attracted me towards a lengthy stand of buff-coloured reeds, all bending in the wind. The sound was so loud it seemed as though the waterfall must soon come into view, but I could get no nearer and trees kept it hidden. Standing, held back by a ditch, I then heard another, breathier sound. Distinct from the roar, it was like a panpipe, although the day had nothing of languor about it. I listened, trying to identify it. The breathy piping seemed to be coming from a gateway – nearer to, from the gate itself.

It was an ordinary metal gate, shut and well secured. Ordinary, that is, apart from having a voice. I stood there, hearing its tuneless but slightly varying note, bemused as to its source, until at last I saw that one of the hollow bars was detached from the frame. It was the wind blowing across its open end that was making that strange, insistent sound.

Whichever drove I choose, there is a hazard towards the end of the walk, in the form of a short section of road without any footway. Drivers take the hilly curves as though pedestrians, cyclists or horses do not exist, so it is an anxious business to walk along there. A public footpath parallel with the road is still marked on the Ordnance Survey map, but has vanished from the ground. Once, only once, a spread of purple orchids growing in the bumpy, litter-strewn verge of the road made up for the discomfort of going that way.

Before reaching the road, if the fields appear to be empty of stock, or only to have sheep, I often walk through them, hoping not to meet the farmer whom I suspect of being padlocker-in-chief down by the anglers' lake. If there are bullocks in the fields, it is a different matter. To be the centre of attraction to a herd of encircling, nosing bullocks is no more enjoyable than having to flatten into a hedge to get out of the way of traffic.

Either way, once two cottages come into view it is but a few steps across the road to the safety of the gate, the track, Ted's sheds and the walk up to the wood.

In winter, when the leaves are down, there is a good view from the top corner of my land where the cedars are growing. But only in times of flood can I make out the river, when it appears in a curling, silver-shining line. The trains are easy to see, especially at night when, like long, twinkling stick insects, they hurry by. It is often getting dark when I walk back from the wood after doing some work, so I need to take the quickest way to the river. The water is good at giving back the last glimmer of light and the path follows the same curves as the river.

But sometimes when I walk back over the moor, especially if in company, it is the pleasures along the way that are the main point. On those occasions, we leave when there is still plenty of daylight, opening up the possibility of taking the slower way back, along a footpath linking Combe to Langport.

The start of this path, to the east of the hamlet, had been taking on a fugitive air. A farm gate lets into a grassy field, but after the footpath sign had gone, and the gate was becoming more elaborately secured, my thoughts turned to the padlocker-in-chief. Was he hoping that this path, too, might fall into disuse?

Once through the gate, it had already been a matter of guesswork where the path lay. The line of a disintegrating hedge had become blurred and irregular, with sheep passing between outgrown blackthorn bushes, snagging their wool on the way. They had made their own hillocks and hollows of the former ditch, in summer drumming the earth of their pathways as hard as brick and linking into one domain their field and a more domestic scene of barn, walnut and fruit trees. Stepping through there felt as much like trespassing on the outskirts of a farm as pursuing a right of way. Which, maybe, was the desired impression . . .

If that was the way things were heading, someone must have been on to it. By December 2014 the footpath signpost was back up, the gate easier to open and a severe shaving had brought the hedge back into line, making it clearer where to walk. It still appears only to lead to a row of trees, but once a small gate comes into view, furnished with robust galvanized latches and springs, it is clear that this really is a footpath.

Next comes my favourite part. The way widens into a green road, with willows and ditches on either side. If it clearly connected a farm with some fields it would be a drove, but it starts and ends too narrowly for that. As it is, it feels like a stretch separated from the present, a way as ways once were, before the invention of tarmacadam. From the west, sunset light sometimes haloes the outlines of cows in the fields, turning the grass to a blazing green and filtering through the willows on to the footpath. It is the sort of path that young Tess of the d'Urbervilles should appear upon, laughing with her companions, not yet heading for tragedy, or perhaps King Alfred, escorting his captive Danes to their christening at Aller.

I hardly ever meet anyone along that path, but it is not overgrown, so people must walk there. One summer afternoon I found myself following a lone brown-and-white cow along it. The cow wanted to walk more slowly, so I was in effect driving it. We proceeded in this manner for a while when, for a brief moment, a scuffling in the ditch distracted me. When I looked up the cow had gone, and in its place a handsome young man was coming towards me. So sudden was this transformation I could not help exclaiming, 'Where's the cow?' He said that he had not seen a cow.

Although this suggested enchantment, that the young man had, but a second before, been a brown-and-white cow, I thought it better not to mention the matter. If the case had been slightly different, a frog instead of a cow, and me only in the guise of a crone, it would have been foolish not to pursue it. But as things were, I gave a more plodding explanation of my question. The prince smiled a winning smile, the westering sun gilded his dark hair, etc., and we continued upon our opposite ways. Curiously, though, I never did catch up with that brown-and-white cow.

Beyond this entrancing passage, the way narrows as it leads out again into open fields. It loops along a raised path beside ditches, with views on all sides across the moor and occasional punctuations in the form of stiles, gates, bridges, glimpses of disused sluices. Willows no longer pollarded splay about in the abandoned ways natural to them, their many fallen branches, still living, piled up upon themselves.

For some years there was an encampment among a group of willows, a sorry-looking affair with a plastic-covered bender and the charred sticks and ash of a fire. When I first saw this arrangement it looked current, so I was curious to see who could be using it . . . children, someone with nowhere else to sleep, vagabonds, rogues forlorn? Year by year the bender deteriorated, its plastic sheets flapping and tearing, till it was just a heap on the ground, then nothing. I guess someone cleared it up in the end, unless every shred of plastic eventually flew, or floated, away.

❧

Soon along this path the railway on its dark-brick viaduct comes into view, with Langport beyond, topped by the tower of All Saints Church on The Hill. Langport's hill is a smaller, less defined version of the several natural tumps rising out of the flat land of the Levels, of which the most famous is Glastonbury

Tor. The Hill is one reason for Langport's existence as a town, a fortified Anglo-Saxon *burh*.

In all the centuries since, the town remained small, hemmed in by wet ground. Now there are new 'traditional' houses going up, tight spaced on any patch thought to be above flood level. In their newness they are noticeable from a distance, but hugger-mugger is the style of the old housing of the town too. If they weather, these outriders may fit in well enough.

At this point the footbridges multiply, as do the disused sluices, the curving ditches and willow-fringed cuts embroidering the land, until the path rejoins the riverbank just short of the railway.

It is a widespread local opinion that, in the current phase of flood-defence engineering, no one knows what they are doing. The old chaps who did know, so this narrative runs, are either retired or dead, and the folly of having reduced maintenance costs for decades is now evident. If this is true, it is not for the first time. In the long history of drainage on the Levels, recurrent siltings-up seem to feature more often than stories of free flow.

That the further reaches of the footpath put the walker in touch with an intricate drainage system is clear; what is less clear is why it is laid out as it is. The rusted screw of one particular sluice gate is still complete with a chain, but it cannot have been turned for . . . for how long? Donkey's years is as precise as I can get. Yet ivy, brambles and fern are only flanking, not smothering, the ironwork, so someone must still be cutting them back. 'BLEY MARTOCK' appears in raised letters on the top. Martock, a nearby town renowned for its Ham stone church and houses, had an ironworks until the 1920s. Even if I were to pursue this line of enquiry, to be able to date the sluice would not date the last time that it had been used. So I revert

sluice gate?

to the donkey's years, and the sense evoked by that section of the walk, of illegible purpose. Illegible, that is, to me. An open book, perhaps, to industrial archaeologists.

Even the new works in progress on one of the local roads have a degree of illegibility. That the road is being made higher is easy enough to understand, and that there should be a new ditch; but why has that ditch been cut out into the field in a looping figure, like a water feature in a garden? Some of the old ditches are also curved; is this throwing-out of loops a way of making a ditch longer, to take more water?

It was a winter Sunday morning when I went nosing around the new roadworks, which were closed to motor traffic. The boy in charge of the Portakabin and, presumably, the security of the site, had his eyes fixed on a screen. He did not look as if he longed to discuss drainage. Lycra-clad cyclists whizzed and a few runners puffed by. There was no one else to pester with questions, so instead I looked out across the sweep of the open, grassy landscape, and up and down the course of the King's Sedgemoor Drain. A few cows, one swan, miles and miles of open land. It was along this very stretch of road, after it crosses the drain and snakes between pollarded willows towards the Aller escarpment, that I had first come to admire and love the Somerset Levels.

For the sake of speed, my original outward journeys from London to Bridgwater had often been by motorway, but there had been less need to hurry back. What a relief, to turn off those pounding great roads and amble gently, sometimes pulling aside to let another driver go past. In daylight the varied greens, the muted browns and greys, the watercolour skies seemed to lap me in comfort. In the grainy dark of night, the car's headlights probed ahead, picking out one bank of willows, then the next, as the curves of the road brought them forwards. Then, it was not comfort so much as something eerie that seemed to be lapping me, courtesy of the illustrations to *The Princess and the Goblin*, with thin, snatching goblin arms reaching out from twisted tree roots.

With the car my cocoon I could slip through untouched, but would not have liked it to break down. I have always driven old cars, and have awaited the cheering lights of rescue vans in any number of different places. But I hope never to do so along there.

Once the footpath from Combe to Langport has made its knotty progress over the waters, the ways part. So long as the ground is dry enough, turning left leads under one of the arches of the railway viaduct to the Eastover part of the town. Prominent among its attractions is a supermarket. Much misgiving went into the decision to allow Tesco to build near the old cattle market, with some people declaring that they would never shop there. But when the store opened in 2002 it was immediately popular. Since then, despite frequent closures and openings among the independent shops, the town has not yet died the commercial death predicted for it. And the willows have grown up round the supermarket, making it less obtrusive from the moor, as though even an outsider such as this can be absorbed into the softness of the landscape, given time.

However, the allure of Tesco rarely diverts me from carrying on along the path to the riverbank, under the railway bridge, back past the sewage works and the lock-keeper's cottage. I do not often gaze at the sewage works but, wanting to look at its bordering cedars, I did stop opposite for a while on one walk. It was 2014, a clear December afternoon, with the sky a glowing yellow. Something was moving. It looked at first like a bobble-hatted head, but when the head disappeared, then reappeared in a rhythmical, repeated way, I saw that it must be a knobby part of one of those revolving structures that are the most recognizable features of sewage treatment, which rotate like playground roundabouts. Starlings were gathering on wires nearby, chattering and flying from one perch to another. Mostly they chose wires that stayed still but, the closer I looked, the more it seemed that some of them were having a go on the roundabout, holding on to rods that led from the circumference up to a central pole.

I was not sure if I was imagining things. At such a distance these playful birds, if that is what they were, appeared only as slight black bumps on the rods, outlined against the sky. The way to be sure was to keep watching, waiting for some of the bumps to fly off. Round and round they went, hanging on tight, despite plenty of movement among their fellows. But after quite a while, off flew one bump, then another. Soon there were no more bumps on the rods and all the starlings were agitating to be off, warming up with a few swirls before leaving the sewage works altogether.

They flew northward so may have been going to join the thousands of their kind that swirl so spectacularly above the reed beds at Shapwick before going to roost. At Shapwick, or elsewhere . . . the time I took friends up there to see this wonder of nature, the only flocks we encountered were of other wishful starling-watchers' cars, the starlings themselves having chosen some other bed of reeds for that particular evening. Now I gather that, thanks to an app, it is less easy for them to evade their human admirers in this manner.

Plodding through mud along the short remaining distance to the garden gate, I pondered how much more quickly the starlings might be accomplishing the miles of their journey over the Polden Hills to Shapwick, if that was their destination. Almost certainly, they would get home before me. Not for the first time in an earthbound life the thought did occur, that arms, wrists, hands, thumbs and fingers may be marvellously useful, but that we did miss a trick when it came to developing wings. If there is a wheel of life and we are able to come back in other forms, I should like to try wings; not, for preference, fine, glistening, swattable wings, but good, strong, feathery ones.

Young
Pear Tree

CHAPTER 10

As Things Stand

There rolls the deep where grew the tree.
O earth, what changes hast thou seen!

ALFRED, LORD TENNYSON, *In Memoriam*

E VERYONE WHO GROWS PLANTS HAS AN eye on
the future, but the tree-planter is particularly given to
looking forwards. With my eye scanning towards 2100,
2200 and a wavering climate, it is easy to see things that could
go wrong for my trees. Not that I fear that the truly deep will
come rolling in upon them in their lifetimes, but the winter
floods of 2013–14 sparkled like the sea only a field away from
the bottom of the track up to the wood.

Some say the floods should be allowed to do so every wet
winter, that hundreds of years' worth of walling, ditching,
draining, diverting, dredging, straightening, pumping should
be let go, allowing the rivers to flood out and the sea to flood
in. But a story from the past does not make that an appealing
prospect. The sea did flood in a big and shocking way not so
very very long ago.

It had been a sunny morning in January 1607. Then huge waves appeared, bearing down on both the south Wales and the north Somerset coasts. The wall at Burnham-on-Sea gave way, letting the water rush in overland for miles and miles, reaching as far as Glastonbury, drowning scores of people and unknown numbers of animals. A print depicting the Welsh side, where things were worse, shows the heads of sheep, cows, pigs, horses looking oddly cheerful as they swim round the tower of a church, with people clinging to trees and housetops and a baby floating by in its cradle. It is unlikely that risking floods on that scale would ever be thought a good idea. Nevertheless, I do feel thankful for land that slopes up towards a ridge.

Floods are one thing, wind is another. Going by the cedars William Pitt planted in the late 1760s on the opposite ridge, wind threatens my cedars more than flood. Pitt started off with a whole avenue of them, but the bigger they grew the more the wind caught them. Only four or five are still growing, some so slim-trunked they look unlikely to be the originals. An even more impressive cedar avenue at nearby Butleigh, planted about a century later than Pitt's, already looks much the worse for the wind, its great and cracking trees rearing up out of the farmland like sailing ships tossed at sea. They form a rather hallucinatory sight as they stretch in a long broken double line across the fields, leading towards a hilltop monument to Admiral Hood.

We already have plenty of wind, but one of the least contentious climatic predictions is that there will be yet more of it. To stand for the centuries I project for them, my two cedars will need good luck on their side. The native trees, oak, ash, hornbeam, may do better in the wind, but then sudden death, dieback, emerald borer, processionary moth and their like keep arriving, either through trade or climate change. Why do there seem to be no good characters in this story, no tree-friendly bugs or moulds or mites hopping over the Channel, or making the most of volatile times?

Meanwhile, without needing any climate change or lapses of international bio-security to help them, undercover voles have chewed clean through the roots of one of my grafted apples. Voles are the suspects because the bigger nibblers were excluded by wire. It was pruning time when this came to light, with the tree feeling loose, then lifting out as easy as the stick of a spent rocket. I felt mortified. Never mind worrying about centuries ahead, I should have kept a clear, less vole-friendly space round the trunk of that young tree during its short present. Instead, concealed under weed-suppressing fabric, those little creatures ate away a five-year sequence, of buying, planting, growing-on the rootstock, taking scions, grafting, transplanting and then rejoicing at the first blossom.

∞

So that the grander trees, cedars, oaks, walnuts, beeches, can go on growing and the fruit trees keep blossoming and giving fruit, the future ownership of the land concerns me. I do not lack heirs, but none so far looks likely to want to take on the work that this patch requires to keep it open, sunny and hospitable to its trees and varied wildlife. I think of old Sir William Pynsent cudgelling his failing wits about who should inherit his estate, even after he had willed it to Pitt, and tell myself I should get something sorted.

Or is it worth it? In dystopian visions of what lies just round the corner, starving, lawless people from a drought- or war-destroyed Elsewhere range the countryside, ownership no longer matters, quaint ideas like nature conservation are absurd.

If the dystopians are right, and the current tragic traffic across the Mediterranean does nothing to contradict them, making plans for the future is a waste of time. However, things may not become quite so bad. With that hope, I contacted a local conservation group to see if it might like to inherit my land.

It was a disheartening process. The first response was positive, but began to career off on a course of its own . . . thank you thank you, and how would you feel if we sold your wood and used the money for the charity? Passing swiftly over that suggestion, I tried to convey that I was not on the point of death, nor eager to relinquish the land, just wanted to put out a feeler concerning its future.

Putting out even a tentative feeler triggered a bureaucratic sequence involving forms, reports, a committee and, as it turned out, a degree of muddle. I was to show someone around the wood, but then that someone was ill so the visit was off. A long silence followed this cancellation. When I made contact again, the first someone had left the organization, so her successor had to ferret about to discover where the process stood.

I assumed that nothing would have happened, but that was wrong. It emerged that another, more important, someone had also had the first date in his diary. Unaware that the visit was postponed, he had gone, had a look and come to some unflattering conclusions. He had reported to the committee, recommending that the members decline my offer. My offer? The feeler had been translated into an offer?

Although affronted that my beautiful place had been found wanting, I asked to see a copy of the report. It started in that sedately affirmative fashion that often ushers in the word *but*, by announcing that the wood was *pleasant* and that *an attempt had been made to dig a pond*. Bridling at that *attempt* and the passive voice, I read on, about the pond having steep banks (bad mark), about the planting of non-native species (bad mark) and how a lot of money would be needed to get the land up to standard, without saying what the money would be needed for. The Rollalong, I was glad to see, got a mention. A friend said I should not be miffed and uppity but should get in touch with the writer to find out about the improvements he thought necessary. Although that may have been good advice, I was not minded to take it.

I do, however, regret having missed the chance to walk around with the report-writer, discussing things as we went. It may not have altered anything, but he would presumably have spoken in the active voice, and I might have found him helpful rather than condescending. But there it is; bureaucratic muddles are part of the stuff of how things happen.

It is doubtless my good fortune that bureaucrats tend to have bigger fish to fry than the owners of a few acres. At the outset my cousin had told me to be grateful that my land had no special designation, of scientific interest, archaeological interest, outstanding natural beauty, or whatever other sort of interest there might be, shale gas, possibly. I have never had cause to disagree with him.

∾

Still thinking of the future, how admirable is Germaine Greer, with her Cave Creek Rainforest Rehabilitation Scheme in Queensland, and the charity she has formed to ensure its continuing wellbeing. Her project and mine are not at all on a par, hers being sixty times bigger, and she being Germaine Greer. But there is one similarity: the wish to ensure that the plant and animal life of a particular patch of the earth will continue to flourish, safe from domineering humans.

Trying to control things from beyond the grave is, however, a chancy business. Trusts can be broken, charities redirected. One recent summer I went to look at three parcels of land up for sale not far from my wood. They were said to be a nature reserve with stretches of open water, no public access, and otters. It was a hot, dry spell, and my leaking pond was so low that the prospect of open water lured me. The land agent spoke in vague terms of a trust, yet the nature reserve was for sale, with no apparent requirement to conserve it.

What a strange, back-of-beyond experience that visit was. Two of the three holdings were alongside each other but the third was separate. None being easy to find, by chance I arrived at the third one first. It lay off the road, along bumpy, axle-threatening droves, where there were occasional signs of activity, of peat-digging, or the amassing of paving slabs, or Guantanamo Bay-type defences round a rectangle of private fishing water. The droves were single-track, so when an old transit van appeared coming towards me, the woman driving it and I had to slow right down to pass within an inch of each other. I lowered the window to ask if she knew where the nature reserve was. 'Yes,' she said, revealing a sketchy set of teeth, 'and it's a right rubbish place, not worth a penny. Mind you leave the car on the corner and walk the last bit, we had to tow someone out last week.'

I saw what she meant, at least about the rutted surface. The separate plot lay over a bridge, thickly enclosed by dark, scrubby trees. If there was open water there, it was invisible. The place felt so gloomy and forlorn I was nervous when a man and a dog appeared, but they both turned out to be amiable. He was an amateur wildlife-photographer, while his dog had the patient air of one used to a life of hanging around. The man was worried about what would become of the reserve, would buy it himself if only he had the money. I related what the woman had said about it not being worth a penny, but he was not so sure. He told me how to find the other two holdings, by rejoining the proper road, then leaving it again a few miles on.

Evening was not far off as I approached the two adjoining properties so, thinking to save time, I ignored the advice about walking the last bit. Though narrower than the droves, this track looked better, at least to begin with. On and on I went in the car, curling between rank fields of weeds on either side towards a stand of tall firs, hoping in vain for a turning place as the surface worsened. I stopped short where the potholes became craters and caverns.

On foot was better. It was a good thing to have bailed out before reaching the trees, because there never was a turning place, even where the agent had put in two temporary bridges to assist potential buyers to cross the ditches. Normally there were no bridges; it really was a reserve for creatures who could manage without them.

It was wonderful in its way, so remote and brooding. Walking towards those firs put me in mind of poor Maggie Tulliver in *The Mill on the Floss* as she, young and hopeful, approaches the Red Deeps to keep a tryst beneath the trees. Maggie Tulliver was not lucky in her men, a circumstance with which I can sympathize. It may be dull of me, but there is some comfort in having reached a stage in life when hopes centre more on meeting an otter than a lover.

The place was overgrown to the point where the promised open water again remained hidden. It was very quiet, as though the birds, of which there must have been plenty, were all holding their breath until the intruder should depart. I crossed one bridge and struggled along a narrow path that looked as if it was only there as temporarily as the bridges, but could see no water.

I might have pushed in further, or tried the second bridge, but the declining daylight hurried me on. It was not the sort of place in which it would have been fun to be benighted.

Wishing the invisible otters well, I walked back to the car, took note of the nearness of the ditches, executed a multi-point turn and jolted back. It was a relief to reach the smooth road in one piece, and with no feeling of desire to become the new owner of such a closed, secretive place.

While I would not agree with the woman in the transit van that those dark and watery lands were rubbish, they were without question more feral than mine. Whether or not they were a better nature reserve, from the creatures' point of view, for being so neglected, I cannot say. Nor do I know why they were for sale or what has become of them. It would be sad to think that they were the relic of a once-beloved project, that someone had died thinking it would all be cared for.

That visit brought to the forefront of my mind an ambiguity about nature reserves: who or what are they for, the humans or the non-humans? Grappling with the thought of my wood carrying on without me, I wonder about that . . . but then I do a Scarlett O'Hara *fiddle-dee-dee, I'll think about that tomorrow* and get on with something more immediate. Setting up some trust or covenant may come later, but for now the trees need to get on with growing, and I with caring for them for as long as possible. I like to think of the indomitable Colette, sitting up in bed in her arthritic old age, planning yet more gardens. *An arbour? Naturally I shall have an arbour. I'm not down to my last arbour yet.* Well, I am not down to my last tree-planting yet either. Not, as I hope, for a long time.

∽

Winter is the time for planting deciduous trees, but winter weather often gets in the way. Planting into frozen ground is not good, but lately at the wood it has been waterlogged rather than frozen ground that has held things up. After my favourite old apple tree fell down, the one with its trunk opened up like a wing armchair, it made a promising space for the tulip tree I had long had in mind. But the two winters, 2012–13 and 2013–14, were so wet that the surface of the ground ran with water all spring and into early summer, so were no good for planting.

I was hoping to plant the tulip tree in the autumn of 2014, but the nurseryman said no, wait and see what the winter brings; after two once-in-a-hundred-year floods running, anything can happen. Nothing much did happen, so on a March day of 2015 in went the tulip tree, as an unimpressive-looking twig. But the twig soon produced lush, ambitious leaves and doubled its height, pushing against the top of its protective wire, so maybe it will make up for lost time.

Several other trees that I had been longing to plant were also held up by those two wet winters, but friends helped me to plant them on the same day as the tulip tree. I have no doubt that some will fit in with their surroundings, a small-leafed lime, for instance, and an aspen, placed so that its white-shimmering leaves will show up from a distance. But I have now got to the point where I worry less about fitting in, so Madame Lemoine, queen of the white double-flowered lilacs, and an ornamental white cherry went it too. I love lilacs, but they take up a lot of space in a garden. Up there in the wood below the cedars, I plan to have a group of them, purple, white, mauve. The sweep of cedar branches may crowd them out one day, but not yet.

Winter work lay, indirectly, behind the story of two of the conifers that are now in that higher part of the wood, near the cedars and larch. I grew them from seed from cones gathered in

Devon. Then some fighting cats muddled up the labelling. One of the trees looks like a spruce, but of the other I am entertaining hopes that it might be something more special.

The winter work in question was a work-creation scheme, brought about in the 1880s by Edward Baring, Lord Revelstoke, to provide employment for fishermen when storms prevented them from fishing. Near Plymouth is a promontory with views out to sea and along the estuary of the River Yealm. Inland, Edward Baring had a big house. For the entertainment of his friends he paid for the making of a coastal carriageway, with stopping-off points for refreshment, so that the guests could be driven around, enjoying the scenery in comfort. He had fine, fashionable conifers planted in a group at one point along this route.

These pleasures were short-lived. A banking crisis, the Panic of 1890, overtook them. The conifers held on, but were approaching their end when I got to know them a century later. In the few years I visited that place, those trees passed rapidly from grandeur to decrepitude (as indeed did Barings Bank, its revival after 1890 seeming to have kept pace with those conifers almost to the day, before they both collapsed in the mid-1990s).

Only at the very last minute did I think of collecting seed from those dead and dying trees, and that without knowing what species they were. When a friend and I scoured the ground underneath them the cones were all splayed open, their seeds gone, and no small trees growing up. All, that is, but one, a tight cone that looked alive. In time it opened up, yielding a few, very few, seeds. On the same day I had collected some cones from elsewhere, from less distinguished-looking trees, just because they were due to be cut down. They too opened up to offer seed. I planted both lots, labelled them, and put them outside.

After quite a wait, these seeds came up looking very pretty, like miniature palm trees. A row of them, a Lilliputian palm beach, stood along the garden wall in London. It was my mistake to leave them there, too close to a cat-and-fox slipway between sections of trellis. By the next time I looked, after some midnight yowling and scuffling, the broken seedling trees were spilt out on the ground, with no way of telling which was which.

In their new, more stable pots, the two survivors started off looking much the same as each other. They grew, somewhat, taking a long time to appear as if they might endure being planted in the wood. When I put them there in about 2006 they were still alike, although one looked stronger. I cannot persuade myself that the one which is now skyrocketing is anything more special than a Sitka spruce, but the smaller is beginning to take on a character of its own. It is darker green, with the hint of a more graceful habit, as might befit a descendant of those carriageway trees.

∾

In responding to this particular fragment of land, seeking to understand something of its past and to have a hand in its future, I am mindful of the risks of nostalgia. Tree-planting looks forwards, but may still express a melancholic sense of looking back, of trying to restore Paradise Lost. I admit that there is not much of the *cutting edge* about working away in a derelict orchard, taking grafts from trees of unknown variety just because they are still there, hanging on. It seems to me that many of the people who have helped me, the sons of farmers and farm labourers, are also holding on, creating forms of rural employment for themselves now that the time of small farms has almost gone, and the production of food is so industrial.

However, I do not at all yearn for a return of the Old Days. Yes, people sang as they worked in the fields and never lacked for company. Yes, some of their descendants look vacant as they wander around Tesco's, and the countryside is becoming more suburban. But still, the old days, as well as being golden, were harsh, harsh, harsh.

The small local-history section of Langport Library includes books of personal reminiscence, some going back two hundred years. Nostalgia might seem an easy pitfall for writers of reminiscence, but much of what I have read is nostalgia's antidote, such is the quality of the lives being recorded, the rough treatment of women and children, the long hours of toil, the overbearing class structure.

One story, of a girl growing up on a Mendip farm before the First World War, was geographically out of my range, but so well written I went on reading. In her autobiography *Beyond the Beeches*, Norah Clacee describes how she escaped the narrowness of her surroundings through a love of books and the chance to leave home to train as a teacher. I was struck by an anecdote she told about her uncle and the local rector.

The uncle was a young man of eighteen. Deep as he was in rural Somerset, he was still able to breathe change in the air, to sense that the old order in which a farm boy showed automatic deference towards supposed superiors was wearing thin. The rector was known for his arrogance and for his love of hunting, shooting and eating rather than for any love of the poor. When Norah's uncle and his farm cart encountered the rector driving his carriage and pair in a narrow lane, the clergyman expected horse, cart and young man to huddle themselves into the hedge. When they did not, in a rage he slashed the youth's face with his horsewhip. And this he felt entitled to do, 'to teach the young puppy a lesson'.

That story held a particular frisson for me because I had a feeling I knew of that rector, that all my life I had, in a way, been eating his marmalade. My grandfather was also the rector of a Mendip parish at about the time of that horsewhipping. Stories have come down to us, along with a marmalade recipe, of a neighbouring rector, or squarson as my father used to refer to him, meaning a mix of squire and parson.

This man was much more squire than parson, my father said, a sportsman and so great an eater of marmalade that he got through a pound of it a day. His wife was required to make the necessary 365 lb of marmalade every January and thus had developed a relatively labour-saving recipe, which she passed on to my grandmother. It is the recipe we still use, although with less sugar. In the shooting season, when not engaged in marmalade-making, the squarson's wife had to deal with the quantities of game her husband brought home. My father made it sound as though she did all this without domestic help, although that seems unlikely.

If the squarson was the same man as the horsewhipping rector, I wonder what my grandfather would have thought of his brother clergyman's violence. My grandfather, a former missionary in India, was all parson and no squire. He and my grandmother were high-minded, Low Church, impecunious and strict, but nothing I ever heard of them suggests an interest in social change, other than conversion to Christianity. Perhaps they would have thought the boy deserved his whipping. I do know from an eyewitness once-removed that my grandmother could walk around her village, commend the good looks of a fine hen, then later find that same fine hen, ready to be cooked, by her kitchen door. Whether she made a habit of this, or it happened once and she learnt not to commend any more fine hens, it is now far too late to discover.

❦

A postcard arrived for me in Langport, on the written side a message from a friend, on the picture side, as I glancingly thought, a pale, scratchy drawing of an *All Our Yesterdays* variety. The friend wrote about being freed from the shackles of editing, but this phrase did not alert me to the nature of the image lying in wait on the other side of the card. When I did turn it over, there, above the caption 'A Peep into Ilchester Bastile', was a scene of torture.

The image showed a bare stone cell, lit by a high, barred window, furnished with numerous shackles and occupied by three men and a woman. One of the men, dressed in long blue coat, red cravat and black, shiny hat, stands by the door, whip in one hand, key in the other. Of the other three the woman appears to be the luckiest, in that only her feet are locked in the stocks, leaving her hands free to be held in an attitude of supplication. She is seated, wearing a green gown, yellow scarf and pale cap, while the two other men are dressed in striped prison clothes.

One man is lying, face upwards, on wisps of straw on an iron cot, chained to the floor by his ankles and waist. The drawing is hard to read when it comes to the upper parts of his body, but there seems to be some kind of binding round his arms and neck. He looks older than the woman, with an agonized face. But it is the plight of the third man that is really painful to imagine. Bent over an iron hurdle, not only are his ankles and wrists shackled together to the ground, even his head appears to be held in a chained clamp.

The man with the whip is not looking at any of the prisoners; his gaze is directed at the viewer. He raises one eyebrow with a nasty, complicit expression, as though including us in the decision, to whip or not to whip? And if to whip, who first? For days after receiving that card, I found myself returning to those unfortunate prisoners in my mind. Ilchester is near Langport, so they might have come from the surrounding area. The likelihood is that they would have been poor.

On the back of the card it says, 'Illustration from A *Peep into a Prison*, 1821, written by the radical orator Henry Hunt, during his imprisonment in Ilchester Gaol.' I later read that it was for addressing the crowd at what was to become the Peterloo Massacre that Hunt was sent to prison. Although he did not complain much about the treatment that he, a gentleman prisoner, received, he was appalled by what was going on around him in Ilchester Gaol.

He wrote his account to expose the brutality and corruption of the gaoler, William Bridle. From cruelty, lechery, embezzlement, drunkenness, falsifying records, hypocrisy to failing to provide fresh water and neglecting the barest minimum standards of hygiene, there was hardly an abuse of which Hunt did not accuse Bridle. A parliamentary commission set up to investigate the claims listened for days and days to the witnesses. Some described a damp, foul, crowded place full of fetters and petty tyranny, others an airy, benevolent Elysium, where illiterates could learn to read and to which inmates longed to return, even when their sentences were over. What the commissioners made of this sterling example of how money talks (it appears to have been taken for granted that the witnesses on both sides would be paid) is not recorded in the transcript of the proceedings. However, to me the chance arrival of this card was a further straw in the wind, a strengthening of the feeling that there are things in this area's, or indeed any other area's, past about which nostalgia is absurd.

∾

Around the time that I was beginning to make some headway with opening up and replanting the wood, someone asked, 'When will your wood be finished?' As with a previous question, 'What is all this for?', I could think of nothing to say. Now I wish I had echoed the aunt who brought me up, who deflected many a tiresome question with 'Wait and see . . .' It is a long wait, many years since I began, and no finishing line in sight. I delayed writing about it, thinking it should look less of a work in progress before being recorded, but have since realized that it will always be a work in progress.

It is not that woods cannot be finished. In fact alarming numbers of them are being finished, every hour, every day, as people spread and the trees are brought crashing or burning down and the creatures among them flee or perish. But being finished, in the sense of being brought to a satisfactory conclusion, is not something that happens in a garden, an orchard or a wood, however well planned or cultivated. I admit that my wood could do with a better finish than it has, with young trees better maintained, hedges better trimmed, weeds better controlled, paths better mown, but as for a perfect, finished state . . . even the best cultivators can only hope for moments of passing perfection, a series of pearls, strung out across the seasons and the years, in between the storms, the droughts, the infestations.

Weather and light have as much to do with these pearly moments as anything pre-planned, worked for. Light, particularly, is a magician. The wood can be looking drear and scruffy for hours when, briefly, the sky to the west clears, letting free the alchemical evening light. Or later, as I walk down the track, the moon may be rising above the ash wood, turning

Ted's orchard into a place of mystery, of shining leaves and dark shadows.

One autumn evening, I had long been back at the cottage but was beckoned out again by the bright moonlight pouring in through the bedroom window. I imagined it would be beautifully reflected in the river, a sort of Moonlight Sonata moment. It was late, but I put on warm clothes and set off.

Out on the moor it looked like the scenery for a ghost story rather than a romance. White in the moonlight, mist was hovering everywhere, clouding high above the river. I walked through it along the bank as far as the railway bridge, with never a hint of moon reflected on water. From somewhere close by came the voices of boys larking about. It made me feel self-conscious . . . boys larking long after dark need no explanation, but what would they think if they met me, not larking but lurking, out on my own?

I decided to take a look around the river bend after the bridge. If there were still no moonlight reflections, it would be time to go back.

As always happens, the turn of the river did offer a change of scene, but only to the extent of showing a faint hint of the moon in the water, more like a dab of whey than a shining silver path. Once back under the railway and heading for home, something must have made me look over my shoulder.

It was not a sound made me turn, because the apparition floating under the bridge came silently, a big, white misty shape. It was startling, but not frightening. Only as it came nearer did the shape resolve itself into a pair of swans. White among white, intent upon their own purposes, they went gliding past. For a moment more I could make them out as they carried on upriver, but then they were reabsorbed into the mist.

The idea of the moon shining on the water still had me in its grip. So, despite it now being clear that the road bridge was the source of the boys' voices, I left the moor and walked there along the street, to see if being on the bridge would help with the moon-watching. If the boys saw me they took no notice, they were too busy being werewolves.

With less mist because of the traffic, the moon's reflection showed clearly enough, a small, irregular white disc on the moving water in front of the pumping station. It looked in no way poetic. I gave up my fool's errand and went home to bed, where my thoughts regrouped . . . those silent swans in the moon-white mist, they were not the clichéd image that I had set out to see. Instead, they were much, much better, unexpected, ethereal, momentary. I could probably stand at the foot of that bridge for the rest of my life, waiting for another such conjunction of moon, mist and swans.

Some of the great pleasure the wood gives me is like that glimpse of the swans, where work and planning are not involved. Instead, it is just a matter of being there.

Even if I think that the question about the wood being finished is, to be frank, silly, the more persistent one, 'What is all this for?', still seems to have some mileage left in it. So I shall try sidling up to it from an oblique angle . . .

At the time of buying the land, I had a conversation with another very old aunt. She was not the aunt who had brought us up, or the one whose fluted teapot lives in the Rollalong, but the wife of my mother's brother, who had long outlived every member of her generation on that side of our family. Like my father, she had had some difficulty in being accepted as an in-law, so she sympathized with him. But, I had heard, the one she really loved was my mother.

This aunt and I were talking in the comfortable care home she was entitled to occupy because of my uncle's First World War naval service. I told her about buying the land, saying that some people thought it a bad idea, but that I felt that my mother might have understood. Her crumpled face lit up. 'Oh yes, she certainly would. Your mother would have loved the thought of a wood,' came her heartening response.

I am not saying that I took on this venture because of a subterranean feeling that my mother would have loved it, but perhaps that played into it. Losing my mother so young, surrounded by private grief but not much communication, I am aware of having created in her image an invisible guide and companion. In real life, daughters and their mothers often quarrel, even part in bitterness, but I was spared any of that.

While I knew her there was never a reason to quarrel with my mother, because she was kindness and good humour itself. She sang around the house, usually forgetting all but the opening words, she loved outings, picnics, gardening, animals, fanciful names. She was always getting, in her own words, 'pixie-led', so that the time flew by and we were often late. She saw good in everyone, or so it sounded. I remember querying why she always referred to acquaintances as 'good Mrs A', or 'Mr B, poor good man'. I wanted to hear how she knew that they were good, although cannot remember her reply.

I know that I have idealized her, but then so did everyone else. When, later on, I would ask the few people left who had known her what she was like, there was no grit in anything they said. It was all smooth and shining, leaving me to wonder how well they had actually known her. But I liked one comment from yet another aunt, a friend rather than a relation, who said, 'You always knew where you were with her.'

I doubt if I took on the wood in order, in some obscure way, to be close to my mother, or to seek consolation for her loss. But to know that we liked many of the same things, being outside, growing plants, loving animals, proceeding in a looping haphazard fashion, is companionable.

When it comes to more bracing forms of comfort, like the need to get a grip, not to let things lapse, I turn away from my mother's example to that of Margaret, the friend who accompanied me to the auction at the beginning of this story. She was a woman who may have matched my mother in kindness but outdid her in clear-headed pragmatism. If my mother was a silver birch, Margaret was an oak. One of the last things she said to me before her recent death was, 'The wood's done well by you.'

Hmmm, thought I at first, isn't it the other way round, me who has done well by the wood? But reflection has reversed that response. Aside from the risk of being cleared, those four tangled acres would have been fine without me, just carrying on their own independent life. But they have indeed done, and I trust will continue to do, well by me. It may not have changed everything around, furnished a belated shining knight, or any other conventionally happy ending to this narrative. But, apart from the joy of being among those particular trees, nettles, birds, animals, insects, it has brought me into warm-hearted contact with many people whom I would not otherwise have met, and been the means of my reconnection with Somerset. It also gives continuing work and hope. Now, having closed my teaching chapter, I feel the value of that.

∾

Leaving aside those white and misty swans and the possibility of serendipitous moments of beauty, my hopes for the wood never included perfection. Not least because that would have meant struggling against the rabbits, deer, rodents, molluscs and, perhaps, smaller creatures and organisms I scarcely know are there. It might have meant the use of chemical herbicides or pesticides, which, it is fair to guess, have never yet been used on that land. Chemicals cost money, and Mr Scriven, my predecessor, was known for his frugality.

Several advisors have said that I should use glyphosate on the coarse weeds, that glyphosate does no lasting harm. But my feeling is, how can we be so sure? I know next to nothing about it, or about the life going on in the soil, so I prefer not to risk putting them together.

This sort of talk drives purposeful people to despair. Good gardeners are often very purposeful, and injunctions to be ruthless or unsentimental are common in garden writing. This makes sense if the aim is perfect control, but my aim is only to reach an accommodation with the wood-dwellers, weeds included. An accommodation such that their descendants, with some of the trees that were there already, plus those of my planting, may flourish together long after I am dead. And for that, I hope, imperfect control may be enough.

In 1999, when my brother first saw the wood in its near-impenetrable state, his comment was, 'Well, it doesn't matter if you don't manage to do much with it, it's lovely anyway,' words that I took as encouragement. If I review what I have done there since, I am pleased that the character of the place, in essence, is the same. The land is more open than it was, inviting in more of the sunlight that falls so generously on that south-facing slope, but there is still little in the way of trees disposed like armies in regular ordination. King Cyrus would not approve, but I like to think that the Genius of the Place does approve, that he, or she, has not been forced out.

Cyrus planted a lot of trees, as do many others who undertake such projects in our own day. Compared with them my count is modest, around a hundred and fifty. Of those, about thirty are fruit trees, while the rest are a mixture of cedar, larch, spruce, oak, beech, ash, poplar, birch, walnut, field maple, hawthorn, holly, cherry, willow, hazel, hornbeam, horse chestnut, dogwood. Some, according to their habit, are already tall, some are biding their time. A few, only a few, never really got going.

Now that I take a mental walk around the wood, it seems that memory and association have mattered as much in my tree-planting as numbers, or the choice of named varieties. The new fruit trees are there mainly in honour of the place itself, with a nod to Sir Thomas Browne, while the cedars are my greeting to William Pitt on the opposite ridge. But most of the planting is more everyday in its connections. There are silver birches, a holm oak, hornbeam and mountain ash, all from seedlings around an inner-London primary school, willows from my cousin's farm, horse chestnuts from Sussex, brought and planted by my late brother, beeches from a Highgate allotment, hollies, oaks, field maples and walnuts from various friends and places.

In 2003 I tried to think of a tree to plant for the centenary of my mother's birth. Both she and my father were gardeners but not, as far as I know, planters of trees. I thought that she might have liked the dark-pink blossom of an ornamental cherry by our front door, but then was not sure who it really was, my mother or my father, who had liked it. I got round the difficulty of choosing a specific tree by thinking of them both as the presiding spirits of the clearing with the cedars.

With my mother's sister it was easier than with my mother, because I knew her for longer. This aunt, the one who looked after us, lived on the edge of a wood. She loved watching squirrels spiralling up and down the larch opposite her sitting-room window. She had also planted a magnolia some way down a bank, with the idea that it would become visible once it grew taller. For many years it stayed the same size. By the very end of her life, too late, it was just beginning to come into view. So I put in the larch and magnolia for her. The larch is racing up, but the magnolia is not. In fact it is declining. There is always that risk, when you grow plants in memory.

∾

After the First World War, the Forestry Commission started planting conifer forests, to make Britain less dependent on imported timber. Down came old broad-leaved trees, up went the conifers. It was very purposeful, but also very unpopular. People were soon complaining about the dreary sight of hillsides clothed in dark green. My father went on complaining about it right up to the end of his life, so I imbibed a generalized prejudice against conifers. Which is odd, when I now consider that the very first trees I was aware of loving were the pines growing in Fisherman's Walk, Southbourne. We lived there in the early 1950s, when it was a busy holiday resort with illuminations along the sea front.

Up in the high branches of those pines lodged the most wonderful creatures . . . owls, squirrels, rabbits, bears, their plastic bodies lit up at night, red, orange, yellow, green. It was the glowing creatures more than the pine trees that stole my heart at that time, but they would not have been so magical down on the ground; it was their appearance high in the trees that I loved.

After London, the first stretch of my regular drive to Somerset is along the M3, where there is a service station set among pine trees. Approaching at night, you see the M of McDonald's, the golden arches, shining high up in front of them. I am snooty about fast food so it took me a while to work out why that sight was such a pleasure. Then it dawned on me that that light, although not coming from an owl or squirrel, was stirring ancient memory. Maybe when my spruce gets even taller I can have a solar panel to power up a glowing golden squirrel, for old times' sake.

∾

ANOTHER PART OF THE WOOD

Every so often, not as often as I could wish, we have had parties in the wood. Parties of one sort or another, a play-reading party, a cello-playing party, a raking party, a damson-picking party, a barbecue. There are parties I would like to have had but which have not happened yet, for instance a snow party. During two winters only has it snowed in the wood since I have owned it, in 2010 and 2012. But neither time could I get there because, ironically, of the snow.

In my mind's eye at least, the snowy wood is sparkling under a clear blue sky, its expanses of white untouched except by the different animal tracks. It is emphatically not the grey-white moody waste captured for me on a mobile phone, the last time I was unable to see it for myself.

For this proposed snow party I do not go so far as to picture skating, because even if it were watertight the pond is not big enough. I do, however, see some tobogganing down the slope, and people round a bright bonfire, the steam rising from their glasses of hot punch. I see, in short, a human version of Margaret Tempest's illustration to *Squirrel Goes Skating*, one of the many Little Grey Rabbit books written by Alison Uttley. She set them on the edge of a wood, and filled them with her love for the old seasonal ways of country life.

Those books have exercised far too great an influence over me. How is one to embrace modernity with Little Grey Rabbit still pattering through the imagination making cowslip balls, Squirrel gathering nuts, Hare setting off with a blunderbuss? The Little Grey Rabbit books were my favourite, but were not alone in giving the impression that childhood and city life had nothing to do with each other. All the children's books we read were set in the countryside, so I concluded that people were only allowed to live in London once they were grown up, which may explain why moving there in my twenties was such a thrill. Now I love both London and Somerset. I never want to leave the one I am in, but am always delighted to arrive at the other.

Parties to enjoy the blossom, or to celebrate the full moon, or leaves falling in autumn, all those poetic parties that sound so wonderful in Chinese or Japanese writing, have also failed to materialize in the wood. I did once attempt a full-moon party in Lord Revelstoke's ruined stone teahouse on the Devon clifftop carriageway, but there was a degree of truculence as we trudged the not-very-moonlit cliff path to get there, followed by sarcasm as the clouds blotted out the moon altogether.

Things went wrong with the play-reading and the cello-playing as well. I had not judged the timing right for the reading. Oberon and proud Titania were able to ill meet each other well enough, not by moonlight but by the milky, midgy evening glow that was still making words legible in the Rollalong clearing. But it was soon too dark for reading, or for gathering up picnic things with any ease, or for seeing rabbit holes. In the case of the cello-playing, the thin sounds we inexperienced late-starter cellists could produce disappeared in between the trunks of the wild plum trees.

I did, however, bear these shortcomings in mind when it came to planning the big party already mentioned in these pages. It happened one June, starting at 5 p.m., in order that most of it would be in daylight but that the guests might stay the course until after dark, as I wanted them to experience the wood both visible and invisible. Not completely invisible, because there were to be many candles in jam-jars and flares along the way. I also asked professional musicians to play, a tango trio and a string duo, on the principle that they would make a good enough sound to be heard out of doors, which turned out to be true.

I consulted with a friend who is a good organizer. His advice was, if you want people to see the whole wood, you have to have something to make them explore, otherwise they will just herd together and drink. So I thought up a trail, with clues that involved traipsing all over the place, beginning and ending at a bivouac of sticks optimistically named 'The Hermitage'.

Inside this bivouac, furnished with table and chair, sat a succession of hermits, taking turns to dress in a cowled cloak. The third of these hermits took to his role with great style, and had even equipped himself with wise saws to pin to the twigs. I was to hear much praise of that hermit. What I did not realize until afterwards was that there had been competition for the job; that a fourth hermit had been awaiting his chance, but never got a look-in. Much as I had dwelt upon things that could go wrong, that problem had not occurred to me.

The days before the party had been wet, the days after the party were wet. I have never stopped feeling lucky that the day that mattered was fine, warm and sunny. I was only regretful that the marquee was standing there, so brave and bright, but more or less neglected. Loitering inside it that morning, looking out towards the south-east, it had felt as though a fine white house, a sort of Southern plantation house, had mushroomed up.

It reminded me of a time when I was escorting some Hackney schoolchildren through the trees at Kenwood, in north London. When the white classical façade of Kenwood House came into view, suddenly a young girl clapped her hands and started dancing round in a circle, shouting, 'It's so beautiful, I want to get married there!' She was of Caribbean heritage, so perhaps she was carrying some folk memory of desirable plantation houses.

The white marquee made me feel something of the same elation, but, grand and spacious as it might have appeared then, it would have been a squash inside if it had rained that evening. Another friend, an engineer, was keen to rig up extra tarpaulins just in case, but really there was no need. The barman had chosen his place outside in the shade of the plum trees, the musicians were happy with the open air, the hermit had his shelter of sticks. All the marquee was needed for was as a dumping ground.

It is good before a party, with the excitement of getting things ready, and even better afterwards. During the actual event I had the occasional feeling of shy detachment, of having taken off to roost in the trees. But most of the time I was right there on the ground, and never more so than at two particular moments.

In one of them I came across an endearing candlelit scene in the Rollalong, in which my brothers were helping my cousin put clotted cream in between the shells of meringues, ready to be heaped up like mountain ranges and carried to the hazel wood for the last part of the festivities. And what meringues . . . so often did I hear afterwards comments along the lines of, nice party, nice wood, FANTASTIC MERINGUES, that there was no choice but to go over to my cousin's and take a masterclass, since when I too can make a fair meringue. My favourite part of her dictated recipe is about the cream. Clotted cream, she says, is far easier to apply than double cream, *in the field*. There speaks a veteran organizer of country entertainments.

But the best moment of all, for me, came when two of the musicians were sitting in the near-darkness on the isthmus of the pond, playing duets for violin and cello by the light of torches strapped to their foreheads. The guests, carrying candles in jam-jars, gathered round to listen while simple, haunting tunes, jigs, gavottes, airs, sarabands flowed out past us into the shadowy trees.

When it was too dark to read another note, even with their miners' lamps, the musicians put away their instruments. The lighted jam-jars started to move off, forming a trembling, flickering line as people made their way up to the hazel wood. That flickering line, something I had not planned, came as an unexpected gift. Like the music, the line of lights was there, but always moving on, until people regrouped to form a glowing cluster. We ate the meringues and cake under the hazels.

Then we finished the party and went home, leaving the place to the trees and the creatures.

And that is how I like to think of leaving the wood. I am only there for a while, a twinkling. But they, and their kind, will remain.

Acknowledgements

Thank you to the many friends who have contributed to the writing of this book. In particular, I would like to thank Sue Gee for her kindness, perspicacity and constant encouragement, Antony Wood and Hazel Wood for their careful reading and sage comments, and Alison Britton for her wit, neighbourly friendship and courage with computers.

I would also like to thank Sophie Scard, of United Agents, and Gesche Ipsen, with other members of the staff at Duckworth, for responding so warmly to the manuscript and working on it with such skill.

My gratitude goes to Penelope Lively for her kind words. Also to Janet Seaton, who researched the archives of Kelway's Nursery and wrote *Kelway's Glorious: The Story of a Pioneering Somerset Nursery* (Picts Hill Publishing, 2011).

I would like to thank my brother and sister-in-law and cousins for being part of the story, and all those who, maybe to their surprise, find themselves included in it. Finally, I am very grateful to my son. Although shy of becoming subject matter, it is he who led me back to the West Country.